# FINDING, LOVING AND MARRYING YOUR LIFETIME PARTNER

*A Practical, Step-by-Step Guide*
*For Men and Women*

Nancy E. Schaumburger, Ph.D.
& Marcia Brinton

**Tudor Publishers, Inc.**      Greensboro

# FINDING, LOVING AND MARRYING YOUR LIFETIME PARTNER

Printed in the United States of America

First printing, October 1988

LIBRARY OF CONGRESS CATALOGING IN PUBLICATION DATA

Schaumburger, Nancy E.
  Finding, loving, and marrying your lifetime partner: a practical, step-by-step guide for men and women / Nancy E. Schaumburger & Marcia Brinton.
      p.    cm.
  ISBN 0-936389-07-9: $16.95.    ISBN 0-936389-08-7 (pbk.):  $9.95
  1. Mate selection.    2. Love.    3. Interpersonal relations.
I. Brinton, Marcia.    II. Title.
HQ801.S436  1988
646.7'7—dc19                                                              88-21055
                                                                              CIP

88   89   90      54321

# TABLE OF CONTENTS

# Chapter One

## GETTING STARTED:
## HOW TO LAUNCH YOUR DREAM

### *Get A Mate, Not A Date*

The right mate for you *is* out there! If you are willing to believe in yourself and take minimal risks, we can help you find this loving person who has been waiting for you. In keeping with the lyrics of Rodgers and Hammerstein, you have held onto your dream in the hope that some day you could make it come true. But if you want to experience the fulfillment of sharing love, you also have to be willing to take intelligent steps toward your goal. To launch a dream, you have to start by proudly acknowledging your deep desire for a life-long commitment and the intention to be selective in your choice of dating partners in order to find this special person.

In a world filled with skeptics, an open admission that you want love which lasts a lifetime can make you feel very vulnerable. You need to remind yourself of the factors which make you want marital fulfillment instead of a "quick fix" to obtain sexual gratification. If you take a good hard look at these factors, you may find that your need to share a committed love, rather than being romantic idealism, is actually rooted in some very practical approaches to reality. You may discover that your dream of mutual fulfillment through marriage is no fairy-tale wish but,

1

in contrast, a very intelligent desire. Mature adults want to be loved, honored and cherished, and to do the same in return. You want intimacy, not isolation. Finding a mate is no panacea for all of life's problems. However, temporary relationships lacking emotional commitment will not provide the satisfying, mature love that you are seeking.

Besides the obvious problems with multiple sexual relationships discussed in high school health classes and further underscored by the current spectre of AIDS, your own experience or observations may have taught you that the "swinging life" lacks genuine emotional rhythm. Not only is there no opportunity for the rich process of individual growth and development, but also sex just isn't as good with people you hardly know. For all that gets touched, the heart is left unsatisfied.

A person who is serious about finding a loving and lovable mate will not find satisfaction in the "rent-a-life" syndrome of serial relationships, or the "marriage of convenience" in which positive feelings and loyalty have long since disappeared. A heterosexual relationship is the most important emotional investment you can make as a mature adult. As you may have already learned, perhaps the hard way, all aspects of your life are affected by the quality and security of your relationship with the primary person sharing it. Health researchers are discovering that an intimate relationship with a loving, committed person of good character as a lifetime partner promotes physical, mental and emotional good health.

## So Where Do You Begin?

Perhaps your every attempt to find a rewarding, permanent relationship has failed. Moreover, you may have been horrified by the "walking wounded" you encountered while wandering unguided in the singles world. This apparently hopeless situation may have tempted you to settle for an unhappy affair simply to have a relationship, or worse, even to have considered celibacy or a permanent solitary state.

The true picture need not be nearly so grim. The search for a lifetime partner can be rewarding rather than frustrating, but you have to develop a trained eye to see the picture within the picture. The first step is to realize that conventional attitudes towards dating, courtship and marriage of the past are either outdated or unworkable. Current American business practices stress the importance of intelligent and efficient choices based upon a systematic analysis of all available facts. Now ask yourself: should not the same intensity of attention and method be applied to finding the person with whom I could live happily for the rest of my adult life? The research and planning methods that have worked so well in the business world can achieve the same successful results in your private life.

Imagine that you are the sole proprietor of a small but thriving business searching for a partner. You would look for an honest, reliable, diligent and amiable person. The needs of your business are unique and, consequently, you need some special assistance in recruiting and screening desirable candidates for the opening you are offering. You might advertise in the classified sections of publications, or enlist the pre-selection services of appropriate agencies. Then you sift through the resumés this advertising engenders, and begin the "weeding out" of unacceptable candidates. A preliminary series of discreet inquiries might precede a few face-to-face interviews with the handful of candidates who pass these early, time-saving stages of screening. Finally, you and the most promising candidate reach a point of perfect satisfaction with each other. You are ready to *go to contract*, looking forward to a pleasant and profitable lifetime of association.

## *Romantic Research*

Why have you gone through all this trouble in selecting a partner? Clearly, you do not want an incompetent partner who might cheat you or damage your business. You want someone who can actively help you realize your goals, a kind of professional help-mate. Shouldn't you use similar discriminating methods to choose a *lifetime help-mate*?

Seeking a marital partner involves the same type of *research* and *planning* that any prudent person would pursue in finding the most advantageous business partner. Such an intelligent search is even more crucial in marriage than in business; marriage, after all, affects *all* aspects of life, not just the eight hours a day you spend earning your income.

This book will show you how to select your lifelong mate and lay the foundation for a good, fulfilling marriage. You will learn how to meet quality people of the opposite sex in comfortable situations which keep *you* in charge of the direction of the relationship. In a step-by-step approach, methods are provided which will enable you to communicate your needs and values effectively in the dating process while avoiding emotional pitfalls. Guidelines for screening potential marriage partners show you how to assess the quality of your relationship from the start and ultimately to select the partner who is right for you.

This book will examine some typical (but false) assumptions many people share which can cause problems in finding eligible candidates for marriage. We will also show you how to apply critical-thinking skills to conduct an effective and rewarding search for a mate. This practical, modern approach can put *you* in charge of your dating situations through guidelines designed to select the best candidates for a serious emotional involvement.

## Plentiful Prospects

Among the myths this book will dispell are the lingering fears you may have that "there just aren't enough prospects out there to make the effort worthwhile." We will demonstrate that "scare statistics" about the lack of available partners are essentially baseless and that the search for a mate can be more rewarding today than at any time in the past. Using updated approaches to dating, we can help you develop a large selection pool of suitable mate-prospects.

## Chance Encounters: A Bad Bet

Another common misconception is the myth of the "Chance Encounter." While occasionally a good marriage may result from this type of meeting, the probabilities can be equated to drawing to an inside straight in a poker game. The idea that two people can meet as strangers and, from that moment on, share a common destiny because of the "right chemistry" is a quaint but harmful fantasy that results from cultural brainwashing. A much wiser approach is the use of intelligent *choice*. We will help you use this gift consciously and selectively to choose the right partner for you.

## Labor and Love: Contradictory Goals

Still another common error is the belief that a chance encounter at the workplace can lead to wedded bliss. Although more women have entered the marketplace and an increasing number of people at work are single, this new opportunity for women has brought with it many complications which make the initiation of dating situations difficult. Signals of interest or availability are not always clear in these settings, and frequently they are inappropriate. Attempts at greater intimacy may result in embarrassment, poor business relations, or even a charge of sexual harrassment. The workplace is often a counterproductive milieu for romantic involvement; office protocols are highly specialized for the purpose of promoting competition and production, not trust and intimacy.

The assumption that you can easily find the ideal mate in your day-to-day activities, such as grocery shopping, is equally erroneous and perhaps, dangerous. Such a belief may lead you to flirt with every person near your age of the opposite sex behind counters, in check-out lines, or even on the sidewalk. Being "on the prowl" every moment of the day is degrading, unrealistic in terms of the hectic pace of our modern daily living, and can even be physically dangerous because you advertise your availability to strangers about whom you know nothing.

## Happy Alternatives

If the traditional methods of finding a mate are no longer effective, what recourse *do* you have? We suggest that you start by redefining your concept of meeting Ms. or Mr. Right from a *chance* encounter to a *choice* encounter. This book will show you how to find and choose situations which are most likely to put you in touch with truly suitable dating partners. As you become more adept at using these suggested methods for selecting potential mates, your confidence will steadily increase until your search will lead you to your ideal lifetime partner.

# Chapter Two

## DEBUNKING THE MYTH OF SCARCITY

### *Scarcity Versus Selectivity*

You may have been intimidated lately by "scare" journalism articles purporting to demonstrate statistically that there is a shortage of marriage partners. Perhaps you're tired of hearing your single women friends complain that all the men they meet at work are married, moronic, or gay. Or perhaps you've heard your single men friends groan all too often that the only women they ever seem to meet at parties are hopeless bubbleheads. What's wrong with this gloomy picture?

It's not that mate-seeking singles are unable to find enough partners—it's that they're having trouble finding the *right* partner. In short, this is correctly re-defined as a *quality* problem, not a *quantity* problem. Remember—you don't have to marry the whole football team or the whole cheerleading squad—*you only need one.*

Your problem is actually selecting the one best person from the many that are available. The numbers are relevant only in the screening process of the search, not in the outcome.

The modern, scientific methods of finding marriage-minded people that we outline in this book guarantee that you will meet an adequate sample of members of the opposite sex. Then, with the help of the tested

7

evaluative techniques we will describe, you can proceed to exercise your human gift of choice.

In short, the problem is *selectivity, not scarcity.*

## *Love Is Not a Lottery*

Moreover, the alarming statistics you may have read in the newspapers need to be interpreted. As you perhaps know from dealings with an accountant, numbers can be made to do amazing things depending on how and where they are placed. Raw, uninterpreted statistics are often meaningless—though they do sell newspapers if they are slanted to look sensational enough.

You should know, for example, that the statistics about the alleged scarcity of singles usually refer only to the *never-married* population—they often don't include the large, ever-increasing "single again" population. When you include this group in your dating, as our methods will encourage you to do, you've already overcome one psychological hurdle—your selection pool is now much bigger than you thought at first. In fact, it may even be *better* also since widowed and divorced people—if they've learned anything positive from their previous experiences with marriage—are often the best bets for a stable, mature relationship.

The "scare" statistics are also insulting to any intelligent, selective person. They contain no information about the *desirability* of members in the opposite-sex group; the only information they reflect is legal eligibility for marriage. Aren't you interested in marrying a person rather than an "eligible"? (If you're only interested in an "eligible" any Skid Row is chock-full of singles! What's more, these unfortunates are sometimes included in the statistics.) Of course you want to be more selective than that. And don't you have more to offer a relationship than your legal status as an unmarried person?

You're no bum or bag lady; you've spent years developing your unique mind and personality. Don't you deserve more than a person with the right sex organs and the right legal document? Hang in there, then, and *maintain your standards.*

8

If you'll look back to Chapter 1, you'll remember that we compared the process of looking for a mate to that of looking for an ideal business partner. It requires research, planning, advertising, expert advice, resumé-checking, phoning, interviewing—a complex, highly active task of screening and evaluating candidates and matching them to the special requirements of the business. In short, it's a *scientific process.*

The statistics you may have read or the discouraging statements of your friends imply that marriage is a kind of lottery, entirely dependent on luck or chance, and there will consequently be a lot of losers. If you are employing the same type of serious methods in mate-seeking that you would employ in finding the right business partner, is it really a lottery? Of course not!

Sitting passively at home waiting for Prince or Princess Charming to beam down on your doorstep may be like playing the lottery—the odds in this case are a million-to-one that you'll lose. But if you're actively searching, scientifically, the odds are excellent that you'll win.

## Scarcity Is Only Local

Let's look more carefully at the complaints of those disheartened singles who claim that all the members of the opposite sex whom they meet are idiots. The crucial question here is: where? At work? At parties? In their whole town?

Even if their complaint includes the whole town, or even a large city, the range of people they have met there is tiny compared to those they could meet if they ventured farther afield. The "shop-at-home" techniques we will outline broaden your prospects to include neighboring towns, counties, states, as far as you're willing to travel to make contact. The frontiers are those *only which you set for yourself*, not those imposed by your location or your limited circle of social acquaintances. (One of the most fascinating mate-prospect resumés we ever saw came from Australia!) You may not want to fly around the world, but you should be ready to meet an interesting candidate at a half-way point of, say, one or two hours travel by car. Consider it to be embarking on an adventure, possibly the greatest in your life.

## Using the Import-Export Method

What did young Chinese men do in the nineteenth century when there was a genuine shortage of females of marriageable age? They imported brides from neighboring countries. What did the Alaskan gold miners do when they wanted women to join them? They advertised for brides. What did many resourceful young British and French women do when there was a shortage of men after the bloodbath of World War I? They emigrated to the colonies, where they were welcomed because of the shortage of women. What do foreign-born American citizens do now when they can't find anyone suitable to marry from their own small ethnic group in this country? They arrange marriages with partners from their home country.

What can we learn from these illuminating and cheerful historical examples? *Shortages are local, not universal.*

How can they be solved? In the same way that shortages are solved in the world of economics—by importing or exporting. It's simply a matter of distribution, not of absolute lack.

The techniques in this book balance out any local shortages of partners in your area by extending your range—in short, by importing others (*desirable* others) and exporting that unique commodity, yourself. These techniques eliminate any regional imbalances which may exist, and maximize your opportunities for selectivity. Both quantity and quality improve dramatically. So congratulate yourself for being a pioneer and proceed on your adventure to the Promised Land of happy marriage!

## If You're Still Worrying, Here's the Clincher

Suppose the worst, that desirable mate-prospects only compose one per cent of the population (actually, by any estimate, they form a much higher percentage). Even if you only have one per cent of the millions in this country to choose from, that's *lots of individuals.* In fact, it's many more than you will ever need to meet in order to make the right selection.

## But What About the Competition?

Most people function at a level of maturity that is far below their chronological age. (We'll show you how to avoid these poor mate-prospects.) On the other hand, you are demonstrating mature, insightful behavior in undertaking a mate-search that is planned and systematic. Your level of development, then, is far beyond that of most of your potential rivals—you have more to offer a relationship. In effect, you're a grown-up in a field of children—you're bound to succeed.

## Only You Will Do

What you have to offer and what you expect to find in a relationship are both unique, one-of-a-kind commodities. *The right partner that you are seeking is also seeking you*—your Mr. or Ms. Right won't settle for anyone but you. Don't keep that lucky person waiting.

## Scarcity May Be in Your Head

We have already seen that the idea of scarcity is not, strictly speaking, a "reality" problem. But what if you still believe that, *on this entire planet*, there is no right marriage partner for you? Then you have a "head" problem.

## Overcoming the Stumbling Block of Low Self-Esteem

If you feel worthless unless you are involved with a member of the opposite sex and hopeless about ever finding one when you are not, you are suffering from low self-esteem. The actual scarcity in this case is not of partners but the unreal scarcity you feel within, your feeling that you lack desirable qualities to offer to a relationship. In short, you feel "unmarketable." If talking to a trusted friend, one who knows and appreciates your virtues, fails to alleviate this problem of negative self-image, maybe it's time to seek some competent professional help.

Low self-esteem sabotages *all* aspects of life. In looking for a mate, low self-esteem often leads to poor screening of candidates and finding yourself unhappily hooked-up with a loser time after time. You owe it to yourself to overcome this stumbling-block to success *before* you become deeply engrossed in mate-seeking activities.

Remember the old saying, "Birds of a feather flock together"? If you consider yourself a loser, you'll attract nothing but losers. You deserve much better—so seek a good therapist first, then an ideal mate.

### What If You're Too Frightened to Start?

Suppose you feel too scared to embark on your search. You know that inactivity insures perpetual singlehood, but perhaps you've never arranged to meet a date in a coffee-shop before, for example, and you're terrified. Is this a "reality" problem or a "head" problem? A little of both, we think. Any unfamiliar activity makes people nervous at first.

How can you minimize your nervousness before you take those difficult first steps? One helpful method is to ask a friend who has already experienced the dating situation that you most fear to describe it to you in detail. This kind of advance preparation familiarizes you with the experience and makes it all seem much less intimidating. In fact, you'll soon feel your anxiety becoming excitement.

Another helpful method of preparation is imagining "the worst possible case scenario." Most people fear being stuck with a date who turns out to be an imbecile, for example. What can you do to anticipate a possible "disaster date"? Always remember to pack your "parachute" in advance (your polite excuse for beating a hasty retreat).

Having prepared for any contingency, you can then relax and enjoy yourself. Even if one date is a disaster, the next one probably won't be. Always remember that there *is* a "next one"—the opportunities are endless.

### You Only Need One

While you are actively engaged in your search for a lifetime partner, you will probably meet many pleasant and interesting members of the opposite sex. You might want some of them for friends. A few could be suitable marriage partners. But you are looking for the *one* individual who is *best* for you. In short, your final task or problem is selection in the midst of plenty, *not* settling for someone who isn't quite right for you because of scarcity. Now what do you do with this delightfully bewildering problem of plenty? The following chapters will help you, by means of refined recruiting and sorting methods, to narrow the many "possibles" to the one "just right" person for you. Remember: you don't need dozens—*you only need one.*

# Chapter Three

## GETTING YOUR ACT TOGETHER

### *Be Prepared!*

Now that you are actively embarked on your mate-search, you should obtain a little special equipment:

(1.) Rent a P.O. Box at the nearest post office. The cost is low. This step will give you a mailing address for many incoming resumés you will soon be receiving from prospective mates and it protects your privacy at home. *Never* give anyone your home address unless you know that person very well.

(2.) Protect your address further by changing your phone to an unlisted number. If your full name is known, your home address can be found in the phone book unless you take this precaution. You definitely don't want strange creatures turning up on your doorstep. (Fortunately, this almost never happens.)

(3.) Buy a telephone answering machine. Some of these are priced quite reasonably—skip the ones with the fancy features. This machine will perform two basic services: it will take messages for you when you're away from home so you won't miss any calls; and secondly, it will act as a private secretary to *screen* these calls. You can tell a lot from a caller's voice message—enough to help you decide whether or not you wish to return the call.

15

(4.) Buy two inexpensive appointment books at the stationery store. One should be carried with you at all times, and the other should be kept beside your phone. You're going to have a very busy schedule!

What have you accomplished so far? You've stopped fantasizing about meeting Mr. or Ms. Right. You've also started to get organized. Now you're equipped for the next step: *specialization.*

To review, don't fantasize—*organize* and *specialize!* Here are the ways in which you, the chief specialist in your own assets and needs, can find the special person who matches them.

### Good and Bad Sources

This section will help you rank good and bad systems of mate-finding just as *Consumer Reports* rates appliances. We will note the advantages and disadvantages of each possibility, beginning with the least-recommended and working up to the modern methods that have been found most successful.

1.  Putting the worst first: singles bars.

*Advantages:* None, except cheapness. (But remember—you get what you pay for.)

*Disadvantages:* Singles bars are notorious for attracting married "moonlighters," alcoholics, and promiscuous individuals looking only for a one-night stand. Moreover, bars are totally *non-selective.* What prior information do they offer about their customers? None whatsoever—no one with the price of a drink is screened out. (The same, incidentally, is true of health clubs—the atmosphere is less seedy, but no one who has the price of a membership is screened out, either.)

This method is also humiliating to anyone who dislikes being ogled in "meat rack" situations. Finally, it's time-consuming and inefficient. Value yourself more highly and direct your energies to better sources. Flee this scene as quickly as possible! It's dumb and can be dangerous. (One exception: University student centers which house Rathskellers and require a student ID for admission may be harmless and entertaining. At least they screen out the street people. However, this exception is still minimally selective—students come in all varieties, from good to ghastly.)

2. *Relatives*. This method of mate-finding is the most traditional.

*Advantages:* It has only one advantage (besides being free): built-in references. You know the relative who wants to "fix you up" is well-intentioned and that the prospective mate is at least a respectable citizen by their standards. The disadvantages, however, are numerous and can be humorous.

Suppose, for example, your Aunt Tillie invites you, her lucky niece Lorraine, over to dinner to meet that "nice young man" Dorian from her office who has "such exquisite taste" in decorating. Dorian, you promptly discover, dyes his hair blond, talks with a lisp, and converses endlessly about his roommate Germaine and their poodle Snookums. You spend the evening trying not to giggle and thinking frantically of plausible excuses for leaving early.

Or suppose your Uncle Marvin invites you, his favorite nephew Jerry, over for a barbecue to meet that "wholesome, outdoorsy" girl Gert, from down at the shop. Gert arrives driving a pick-up truck and wearing a black leather jacket. She outweighs you by 100 pounds and consumes five hot dogs and three quarts of beer. You spend the evening hiding behind a tree.

Or suppose your cousins Josephine and Henry invite you over for tea to meet that "nice, old-fashioned girl" Lucy from their church. Lucy turns out to have no interests other than darning socks and talking to her parakeet. She is "a little shy" to the point of schizophrenic withdrawal. You have spent more stimulating afternoons with a potted plant. Suddenly you remember an important appointment with the tax auditor.

The left-over problem from these three types of "disaster dates" is how to face your kindly relatives over the turkey when Thanksgiving rolls around. What can you possibly say?

This method of meeting people is not highly recommended because it is both unproductive in most cases and loaded with 'fiasco potential.' Unless you share the same values, standards, and perceptions as your relatives (a very rare situation nowadays) this method is probably a waste of time.

What about friends as a referral source? There would seem to be more hope for this method because your friends are chosen and more likely to reflect your own interests and preferences. However, there's still a lot of fiasco potential lurking in this source of blind dates. Why?

What secret motives do both relatives and friends have in common when they try to fix you up? Usually they are trying to "unload" a socially hopeless acquaintance whom they have semi-adopted. They are trying to divide the burden of helping this poor John or Jane with someone else—you. Our advice: Do a polite but speedy side-step.

*3. Social clubs* with background requirements offer a lot more selectivity.

*Advantages:* Here the watchword is, *the more specialized the club is, the better it is.* For example, a Jewish singles discussion group narrows down the membership to a small degree. But, see how much more selective this one is: a singles group for Jewish social workers aged 25-40 who are interested in bird-watching and back-packing activities. Now, that's specialized!

There are all sorts of social clubs organized around all sorts of common denominators, or "magnets"—ethical, religious, professional, hobbies. Do what the Yellow Pages tell you to do: "let your fingers do the walking" (or, in this case, the pre-selecting) for you. Check the phone book, club announcements in the newspaper, church and temple bulletin boards, and so on.

Some social clubs you might want to consider are: Kindred Spirits, Parents Without Parents, and Widows & Widowers groups. Many towns have branches of such singles social groups, plus many others.

What if there are no "magnet" social clubs of this specialized kind in your area? Take the initiative: start one! Put an announcement in the paper or post some on a few likely bulletin boards. You'll soon find that there are others who are seeking the same common-interest type of meeting ground.

*Disadvantages:* There may be a membership fee, small or large, depending on the nature of the organization. It could be worthwhile. Social clubs do offer fun and friends of both sexes, if nothing else.

The other disadvantage is that social clubs eliminate the useful prescreening stages of resumés and phone calls—they catapult you right

18

into face-to-face meetings. This method, then, is not the most careful or the most efficient. It is best to use it in combination with other, more focused types of approaches.

4.   *Advertising.* Putting an ad in the Personals column of a newspaper, magazine, or "dating guide" used to be regarded as a daring, even disreputable thing to do. Now millions of people do it regularly as an effective way of making contact with large numbers of the opposite sex.

*Advantages:* It's active, safe, convenient, relatively inexpensive, repeatable and high-yielding in responses.

*Disadvantages:* Advertising offers few pre-selection features. It produces quantity, not quality. No matter how respectable the publication you select or how carefully you word your ad, you will receive dozens to hundreds of replies from kooks, crooks, and people who have nothing in common with your interests. However, you may also find some "pure gold" candidates if you wade through this pile of mail. It's a worthwhile starting point. Some "regulars" swear it's the best method because of the sheer volume of responses it generates, but we rate others more highly.

5.   *Professional Matchmaking Services* of the walk-in type. These services, which are proliferating rapidly nation-wide, can be found in the Yellow Pages, in newspaper ads, and in radio and TV commercials. They usually involve one or more of these three techniques: (a) filling out a questionnaire on your interests, likes and dislikes; (b) being recorded on videotape as you chat with an interviewer about yourself and the kind of mate you are seeking; and then (c) leaving this material on file at the office for any interested members of the opposite sex to look over. (Sometimes "computer matching" is used to help people get together. This can be anything from a real computer match of thousands of names to some clerk riffling through a batch of cards and putting together the ones that look good.) Some company names in this are Introlens, Together, Great Expectations, Matchmaker International, Godmothers Ltd., and People Resources. There are *many* others—you should check to see what's available in your area.

If you become a member of one of these clubs, here's what will happen next: someone views your file and finds it appealing, then contacts you by letter or phone, as you prefer. You, too, have the privilege of looking up and initiating contact with other members (up to a certain maximum, usually under ten selections).

*Advantages:* This method is safe, cautious, convenient, dignified, and fairly selective. It also offers a guaranteed minimum of introductions to people you select yourself. It's basically a "shop-at-home" catalog for the discriminating mate-seeker. *Reservations:* Sometimes the questionnaires are not sufficiently detailed (learning only that a member is a non-smoker and an accountant who likes to jog, for example, tells you very little about his or her personality and nothing about his or her past). Sometimes the interviews are similarly superficial, ("Tell me, Charlie—do you prefer blondes or brunettes?").

*Disadvantages:* It's expensive! Depending on the degree of personal advising and the exclusiveness of the organization, the cost of membership for a few months or for a year can range from $250 to over $3,000. You may not wish to spend so much money. Worse, this method eliminates too many desirable mate-prospects who can't afford the service.

Perhaps, then, matchmaking services of this type are helpful if you can find a reasonably-priced outfit in your area, and use it in combination with other methods.

6. *Professional matchmaking services of the "magnet" type* that operate by mail. Examples: Single Booklovers, Classical Music Lovers Exchange, Health Conscious Connection, Music Lovers Matchline, Art Lovers Network, Bibliobuffs, Singles Scene (for Christians), Personal Search, Electronic Exchange, Dating for Disabled (for handicapped singles), Identity, and many others.

These organizations attract members by advertising in respectable periodicals such as *The New Republic, Psychology Today, The New York Review of Books,* and others. (Some ads run in national publications, some local.) These groups or clubs are organized around common interests, achievements, or ethnic identities of all types. They usually have a nationwide clientele, but some are regional.

For example, some groups are aimed at art lovers, movie lovers, outdoors lovers, gourmet food lovers, tennis lovers, theater lovers, pet lovers—you name it, there's a group organized around it. The key word in the name is often "Lovers" but there are also groups named "Exchanges" or "Networks." Other types include single college graduates, "super-achievers" (people with advanced degrees), professionals: Jewish professionals, Christian professionals, Greek professionals, and many other specialized variants.

There are even groups for single people with special problems, such as learning disabilities or other handicaps, and for people with special life experiences, such as widowhood.

Once you have found an ad for a club that appeals to your interests, you send for an application and receive a Membership Profile sheet (a kind of resumé form which elicits detailed information about your background, personality, cultural interests, likes and gripes, and other significant data).

You submit your profile, which is kept on file, and you receive a newsletter each month listing all members of the opposite sex by an identifying number (*not* by name), city, state, and three-line self-description.

If any listings interest you enough to seek further information, you may request their profiles by number. When you receive the profiles, you study them carefully and decide which ones you want to contact by letter, phone, or both.

*Advantages:* It's relatively inexpensive, usually under $50 for a six-months' membership, plus about $3 for each profile requested. Better still, it's the *most highly selective and convenient method* currently available. It puts you in the driver's seat—you shop-at-home completely during the preliminary stages before face-to-face contact (as opposed to the walk-in matchmaking services). *You* make the selection, *you* initiate as well as receive the contacts by mail.

*Disadvantages:* Only one—very minor. You need a little guidance in writing an effective profile and "decoding" the self-descriptions of others. The next two chapters, HOW TO PREPARE A PERSONAL RESUME and THE DISCRIMINATING DECODER will show you how.

21

## Should You Use Only One Method of Meeting?

In our experience, method number 6 is the best. However, if you want to be *absolutely sure* of meeting large numbers of people, you may also wish to try methods 3-5 for a couple of months. It's possible that you'll have some pleasant dating experiences with other methods before you settle on the one method of mate-seeking that's most productive for you.

If you've now become a member of Single Booklovers or Classical Music Lovers or any other interest-oriented club that operates by mail, should you limit it to that? We suggest the *buckshot approach*—join as many suitable ones as you can afford. After all, locating the marriage partner of your dreams is probably the most important investment of time you can make. It's worth spending a little money, too.

You'll be able to decide, after a short period of experimentation, which clubs produce the best quality for your personality. Then you can drop the other memberships. Meanwhile, you're going to be *very* busy dating and having fun as you and your ideal mate move closer to finding each other.

Now turn to Chapter 4 and start filling in your resumé. This is where the search really takes off.

# Chapter Four

## HOW TO PREPARE A PERSONAL RESUMÉ

### *"Know Thyself"*

You have selected one, or several, singles organizations which appear consistent with your personality, interests, and goals. You have received general information which includes instructions regarding a short self-description and a personal profile form which will be distributed among the membership. However, before you embark on this pioneer journey, you have a crucial preliminary step to take.

Previously, in discussing the recruitment of business partnerships, we stressed the importance of focusing upon the features which were most likely to bring about the desired results. Recruiting a mate involves many of the same principles, but this most intimate of situations requires much more personal and introspective exploration. Therefore, in the words of Socrates, which still hold true today, before beginning this new experience you must first "Know Thyself". You must refine and clarify your own desires, needs, aspirations, and responsibilities before you can communicate them to others or expect the person you eventually choose to help you fulfill them.

Let's look at the most important issues you must investigate within your personal domain which will affect your selection of a mate, and the kind of interdependency you can develop together. The first set of

23

critical factors involves self-esteem, personal values, and expectations of intimacy in a marriage. The second set includes attitudes toward family—children, parents, other relatives and close friends—who need to be incorporated into the primary relationship between a wife and husband. The last factors include expectations in lifestyle.

So, before you write anything on a personal profile form, use a separate sheet of paper, or a tape recorder if you talk more freely than you write, and diligently answer the questions below. Take all the time you need and be completely honest. Unlike newspaper or magazine questionnaires, no one is scoring you according to the latest trend. There are no right or wrong answers. There is only information—critical information—about your deepest, most cherished hopes and dreams.

You may experience a great range of feelings in performing these exercises. Some may be upsetting. Be gentle and nurturing to yourself, take as many breaks as necessary, and bounce your less-developed ideas off a trusted friend or relative if this helps you clarify your confusion. But, whatever it takes, stick with the task until completed and you are satisfied you have accurately captured yourself—*who* you are and *what you want* in a life relationship.

## Warm-Up Exercises for the Big Step

Relax, take a deep breath and give your best effort to the following questions to clarify your attitudes about yourself, your personal beliefs, your ideal mate, and your values about marriage and family.

Self-Image and Personal Beliefs:

1.  What kind of person am I?
2.  What do I like best/least about myself?
3.  What would I be willing to change? How would I accomplish this?
4.  What moral values do I value most (e.g., honesty, kindness, generosity, etc.)? Do I have any double standards for myself vs. others?

24

5. Are my values absolute or do I judge them in context with the situation?
6. Have my values been beneficial or limiting to me? If so, in what way?
7. Are my values worth keeping and defending even at the cost of ending a personal relationship? Which ones? Do I feel some of them should be changed? If so, which ones? How would I accomplish this?
8. Do I have a basically optimistic or pessimistic view of the human race in general? Why?
9. Do I separate people into groups I like and dislike? If so, what criteria do I use? Why? How helpful or limiting has this been for me?
10. Are there attitudes toward others I wish to change? If so, how can I accomplish this?

Attitudes About Intimacy and Marriage:

11. What characteristics do I have which would most help or hinder a mate? Is there anything I should, in fairness, change for a mate? If so, how would I accomplish this goal? Are there perceived strengths I would retain even at the cost of ending the relationship? If so, what are they? How well do I communicate these values in dating situations?
12. What characteristics and behavior do I want in a mate? Are they similar to my own? Why (why not)?
13. What are my feelings about heterosexual intimacy? Do I want mutual self-disclosure, and the sharing of deep feelings, to occur frequently, occasionally, or rarely in my marriage? Do I want to have sex with my mate frequently, occasionally or rarely? Do I want affection and devotion—verbally and behaviorally—expressed frequently, occasionally or rarely?
14. What steps do I expect to be followed before permitting greater intimacy or making an exclusive commitment? Would I expect a prospective mate to want similar steps followed? If so, why? If not, why not?

15. Do I want to have children with my mate? Would I be willing to forego this experience? Would I be willing to help raise a mate's children from a previous marriage on a full-time or part-time basis? (If I have children) what role would I expect a mate to take in their lives? What kind of commitments and support would I expect a mate to make on their behalf emotionally and/or economically?

16. Would I be willing to maintain a relationship with a mate's parents, other relatives, and close friends, attend or host family functions, etc.?

17. Would I share the responsibility of providing care directly or indirectly for a mate's parents when they can no longer take care of themselves?

18. What type of lifestyle do I expect in marriage economically and culturally? How much am I willing to contribute and how much do I expect my mate to contribute? How equally is the responsibility divided?

19. Do I expect similar or different gender roles between my partner and myself? If different, how do I propose to maintain fairness and equal power in the relationship?

20. How much time do I expect my mate to allow me for pursuing my own separate endeavors? How much time do I intend to allow my mate? Are my expectations for my mate and myself identical, fairly similar, or significantly different? What is my rationale for my position?

## *Zeroing In On Key Issues*

When you've finished these questions, you will have a wealth of information about yourself and all that you hold most near and dear. You are now ready to focus on the key areas which best convey your personality, philosophy, and goals. Although you will use only a condensed amount of this overall information, you should save this larger body of self-knowledge for future use when you reach the stage of decoding other personal profiles, of dating, and of exclusive commitments.

One important word of caution: in reviewing your answers to the questionnaire you should make special note of any contradictions or wide discrepancies in your statements. These are red flags for *conflict areas* within yourself. You may need more time to work with these areas before proceeding further, because they can sabotage your most sincere and diligent efforts.

Unresolved conflicts can also hurt others despite your kindest intentions. Dissatisfaction and 'double-binds' caused by these conflicts may harm a relationship. One such classic case is the "doctor's wife" who wants the status of her husband's profession, but is unable to tolerate the demands made upon him by others. Another example is the man who feels he has outclassed the rest of the pack by marrying the gorgeous model everyone is ogling, only to find that he is incessantly jealous because her career demands that she continue to be publicly ogled. Yet, in each case, if the partner succeeds in getting the mate to change careers, the marriage is just as doomed. The unhappy partner remains unhappy because now the mate no longer possesses the specific status of "doctor" or "fashion model" which was originally so attractive. Unfortunately, everyone close to them is also drawn into the misery.

You can avoid these tragic outcomes by being honestly aware of unresolved conflicting desires and getting to their source through self-examination, counseling, or psychotherapy before making yourself and another more unhappy in an unhappy relationship. If, for example, a woman who loves conversing about a wide variety of topics, impressions, and reactions wants a man who is the "strong, silent type", or a man states he wants "an independent woman with old-fashioned values," the obvious conflict means that the failure is inevitable. Contrary to pop-culture myths, relationships are not cure-alls for confusion about self-esteem, values, responsibilities to others or social expectations.

## *What They See Is What You Get*

After clarifying your own attitudes, values and expectations, you are ready to write a rough draft of your personal resumé. Here it is important to be as specific and succinct as possible. Remember, unlike those terrible teen years, it is no longer necessary to worry about how popular or "with it" you are. You are not interested in marrying the majority of the eligible population. You seriously seek *one* person who is able to be and wants to be the right mate for you. To attract people for your selection pool, you should indicate and look for similar philosophies, tastes, and interests.

The more vague you are in filling out your personal profile, the greater the fiasco potential. For example, a woman indicates that one of her favorite forms of recreation is "hiking in the wilderness" because every Sunday afternoon she dons her tweeds and binoculars for a bird-watching walk in the woods. She may be dismayed by a date who arrives with equipment for a survival excursion to Alaska and the expectation that the two of them can build their own igloo at the edge of a glacier.

Being very specific not only reduces fiasco potential, it enhances opportunities for conveying your special qualities and capacities which can be recognized by a kindred spirit. This is particularly true in cultural areas in which people's taste often reflects their deeper personalities.

Preferences in art, literature, and music may be important indicators of a person's needs regarding sensitivity, levels of introspection, and esthetic appreciation. For example, an individual who lists his or her favorite book as *The Brothers Karamazov* or *The Fall*, both of which deal with complex psychological, social and moral dilemmas, is also communicating that he or she is more introspective and intense than someone who lists *Rebecca of Sunnybrook Farm* or *Pollyanna.* Devotees of Bach may prefer an innocent, harmonious emotional environment, while those who most enjoy Mahler may thrive on more emotional contrasts and mood swings.

These areas of interest, therefore, may provide subtle information about your personality which, in conjunction with other self-statements, are helpful to a person of the opposite sex who is trying to make a serious search of his or her own.

## Examples of Well-Drawn Personal Profiles

Let's look at two sample resumés in which the individuals successfully communicate key facts about themselves. Sarah, 31, who has never married, holds a B.A. in English and works as a circulation director for a publishing company. In applying for membership to Single Professionals, she responded to the categories involving interests and personal philosophies as follows:

- Interests in marriage (great, moderate, slight, none): *moderate*

- Religion: *Reformed Jewish*

- Favorite books: *Anna Karenina, Jane Eyre, Portnoy's Complaint*

- Taste in plays: *Usually off-Broadway with a message*

- Favorite outdoor sports: *Sailing, swimming, volleyball*

- Favorite magazines: *New Yorker, Psychology Today*

- Taste in movies: *Love Woody Allen! Fellini*

- Taste in music: *Classical, ragtime, jazz*

- Three things which you dislike in today's society: *The me-first philosophy, instant gratification, superficiality*

- Three things you like most: *More career flexibility, more employment opportunities for women, more international communication and flow of ideas*

- Traits you dislike most in others: *Narrow-mindedness, selfishness*

- Traits you like most in others: *Creative curiosity, concern for others*

- Characteristics you consider most important in a prospective mate: *Integrity, honesty, dependability, an interest in cultural things—art, music, books, sensuality*

- Additional information about yourself that you want a member of prospective date to be aware of: *My roots are in Northern N.J., not interested in a pen-pal or long distance relationship, not interested in one-night stands. Looking for a mutually supportive relationship with shared interests*

29

Let's look at Brad's responses to the same singles organization. A former political science major as an undergraduate, Brad, who is approximately the same age as Sarah, now works as a marketing manager for industrial products. He is divorced with two children, and an involved parent though the children do not live with him. He cites his interests and values as follows:

- Interest in marriage (great, moderate, slight, none): *great (with the right woman)*
- Religion: *Congregationalist*
- Favorite Books: *The Third Wave, Lake Wobegone Days*
- Taste in plays: *Miller, Shepard, Neil Simon*
- Favorite outdoor sports: *Tennis, skiing*
- Favorite Magazines: *Wall Street Journal, New York Magazine*
- Taste in Movies: *Everything from Mel Brooks to George Lucas*
- Taste in Music: *Light classical, jazz*
- Three things you dislike in today's society: *pollution, apathy, forced retirement*
- Three things you like most about today's society: *Adult education, greater involvement of men in child-rearing, more progressive thinking*
- Traits you dislike most in others: *stubbornness, irrationality, irresponsibility, being a bore*
- Traits you like most in others: *A sense of humor, intelligence, flexibility, fairness, assertiveness*
- Characteristics you consider most important in a prospective mate: *same as above, warmth, and enjoyment of children*
- Additional information about yourself that you want a member or prospective date to be aware of: *I'm a friendly, outgoing person, looking for someone with the same approach to life*

30

An examination of both Sarah's and Brad's personal resumés illustrates two very different personalities. Their profiles indicate that they are mature, responsible, concerned with others, and interesting. Yet each cites individual preferences which are unique.

Sarah makes it clear that, in addition to good character, she needs cultural outlets for fulfillment. She also attempts to ward off deceitful, undependable men rather than having to encounter them in person. Although her tastes and self-statements indicate that she is no prude, she is very specific about her desire for a serious heterosexual relationship rather than casual sex or platonic friendships. She also communicates that she has made a pleasant lifestyle for herself, has developed close ties with others over time, and is probably unwilling to relocate.

It is unlikely that a man wishing to be Sarah's date would consider attempting to subordinate her life to his. In contrast, he will most likely be the type who wants an egalitarian relationship with a successful, cultured, sensual woman.

Brad communicates that he is a solid citizen who also insists upon good character in a prospective mate. He highlights the fact that a positive relationship with his children will be a critical selection feature. In contrast to Sarah, Brad does not need "highbrow" tastes for his desired lifestyle, but he does need shared outlets involving current ideas, sports, recreation, and entertainment.

His statements will most likely discourage clinging vines, airheads, or Motel Mollies. By being specific in a number of areas, he is likely to interest mature, nurturing women with a capacity to enjoy life and a well-developed sense of their own worth.

## How Accurately Have You Painted Your Self-portrait?

When you have finished the rough draft of your own personal profile, look it over to determine whether it presents a unified picture consistent

31

with the broader 20-question inventory about yourself and marriage you grappled with earlier. If you have been true to yourself and specific in communicating your interests, abilities, values, and desires, you should be pleased with the results, and proud of being who you are.

Your resumé should now capture your overall purpose and intention in making yourself available for dating within the specific organization you are joining; you want the opportunity to meet *suitable* dating partners according to your standards, people with the potential to become suitable *marriage* partners. The last details consist of recopying the form or forms and writing a brief (approximately three-line) self-description to send with the profile.

Sarah's and Brad's short descriptions, which are fairly standard examples, may be helpful as guidelines for your own:

> Female, age 31, single, 5'5", circulation director, settled, secure, loves good literature, plays, music, art and Woody Allen films. Seeking mutually supportive relationship with shared interests.

> Male, age 35, divorced, 5'10", marketing manager, two children, friendly, outgoing, interest in companionship with someone similar, likes intelligent discussions, tennis, skiing, movies, current books and plays.

Many organizations also encourage descriptions of one's physical attractiveness. Moderation is the best guideline to follow in providing this information. Most people are attractive by conventional standards. Whether you are a knockout and know it, or feel yourself to be less attractive than you would like, it's generally better to de-emphasize your physical appearance and stress instead your other assets and accomplishments to attract a desirable, nice person who is looking for more than a pretty or handsome face and physique.

If you are in poor physical shape or have neglected your basic grooming, you may want to improve these areas because it would be better for your own health and self-esteem. You would also be more true to your overall goals for a lifetime relationship, because problems in these areas are not the most desirable attributes to offer a mate. However, you do not need plastic surgery, exotic make-up, or glamorous health spas to be qualified for love, respect, and commitment.

## *Countdown Ended—The Dream Is Launched*

With your profile in the mail, you've completed a pioneer achievement which will change your entire life. With your own initiative, you've traversed the huge hole left by your culture when it went catapulting into a high-tech age. You've generated a method for signaling your availability for a serious relationship with prospective candidates by communicating the important facts which make you unique and compatible for the right individual. You owe yourself a pat on the back and a toast to your courage and initiative.

The following chapter will discuss the next step—how to make the best selections based upon the personal information provided by others. However, before reading on you might consider taking a short break and resting on your laurels. For getting this far, you deserve it!

# Chapter Five

## THE DISCRIMINATING DECODER

### *How to Decode Personal Ads and Singles Club Bulletins*

When you set about the sometimes confusing task of determining the "real" message between the lines of a personal ad or three-sentence self-description in a singles club newsletter, the first feature you should evaluate is the nature of the publication. In the case of the singles club newsletter, you already know a great deal because of built-in pre-selection features (a member of a club such as Single Shakespeare Lovers, for example, probably does read books and enjoys drama; otherwise he/she would have joined some other club). The only information you need to decode in this case to determine whether it's worthwhile to send a profile is that pertaining to personal traits and habits.

Personal ads in newspapers or periodicals are a little trickier, but they too can reveal a lot about an individual's educational background, aims, and financial status. For example, tabloid newspapers of the more sensational varieties are usually a poor source. They tend to attract advertisers who are less sophisticated, less affluent, sometimes farther away from your hometown, and often more kinky than the people you would like to meet. So if you wish to avoid the "tattooed ladies" and other strange breeds who advertise here, push on to better sources.

## Where to Look

There are three chief indicators of a good publication for single advertisers and readers:

1.) It should be local rather than national. You want to meet someone nearby, after all, not three states away. City-based or county-based magazines that feature articles on dining out and other leisure activities are the ones for you. Examples for singles in the New York area: *New York Magazine, Westchester Week, New Jersey Magazine.* The readers of such magazines are usually socially active, literate, and near enough to meet. These are also smart places to advertise because such publications have a longer circulation life than a week or a month; they continue to be read in dentists' waiting rooms for a half-year, attracting the attention of alert readers like yourself.

2.) Moderately highbrow publications such as book reviews are usually better than picture periodicals. Their advertisers are usually well-read, up-to-date people.

3.) Specialized publications, such as professional newsletters and some corporate magazines, are often excellent because they target people who have had experiences in common (the nature of their work, and frequently their education or training). While it's true that these publications have a more limited audience than the bigger, glossier types, they offer perhaps the most reliable pre-selection features. Don't overlook them. (One of the happiest marriages we know resulted from a personal ad in a professional librarians' magazine!) Hobby-type magazines, such as those which focus on camping activities, are often a good source also.

Again, the leading rule is: *the more specialized, the better.*

## What to Look For

Before you can read between the lines of a personal ad or club-member's self-description, you need to know the usual abbreviations. This part is easy. All ads begin with information about sex, race, marital status, age, and sometimes religion. For example, DWM, 35, means divorced white male, age 35. SJF, 22 means single Jewish female, age 22. DBM, 43, means divorced black male, age 43. These abbreviations are standard. The only abbreviations you should avoid as definite danger signals, or "red flags," are "S&M" (interested in sado-masochistic sexual activities) and "bi" (bi-sexual). Armed with this information, you are ready to proceed to the rest of the ad. Here are some practice examples:

DWM, 36, lawyer, father, old movie buff, seeks cultured lady to share VCR, concerts, beach life. P.O. Box 111.

Should Sharon answer this ad? She too is a professional and a parent, she enjoys the quiet activities that this DWM names, and she too is *seeking a mate, not just a date.* This is a clear "yes".

SWF, 27, cosmetics executive, "JAP" and proud of it, seeks gentleman to share sailboat, dining, the finer things in life. P.O. Box 222.

Should Paul answer this ad? He's the right age, never married, and enjoys sailing, but this SWF indicates no interest in a permanent relationship. Moreover, he's suspicious of a woman who proclaims even humorously that she is a "JAP" (Jewish American Princess, a stereotype of spoiled, materialistic femininity). Paul is a struggling graduate student who couldn't—and wouldn't want to—satisfy this SWF's expensive tastes. This is a definite "move on".

SWM, 30, Boston-based sales rep., varied interests, seeks Philadelphia girl for dancing, nightclubs. P.O. Box 333.

Should Daisy answer this ad? She does enjoy dancing occasionally, but she's a secretary with small children and looking for a stable relationship. This SWM wants a carefree companion for dates on an irregular basis (he lives out of town, and may even be married). Daisy wisely decides that this ad is suspicious and moves on.

DWF, 35, assistant editor, 2 great kids, 3 uppity cats, broad cultural interests, warm personality, seeking compatible fellow for friendship, fun, talk, life. P.O. Box 444.

Should Barry answer this ad? He too likes kids and pets and has a few of his own, he enjoys all cultural activities, and prefers warm, affectionate, upbeat people. Moreover, this DWF is clearly seeking a *mate, not a date*—as Barry has been doing himself for several years. Here we have a definite "yes".

SWM, 41, gynecologist, seeks petite blonde with lots of style for yachting, traveling, the good life. Share an adventure with me! P.O. Box 555.

Should Norma answer this ad? She happens to be 5'2" and blonde, but she feels she has a lot more to offer besides her physical appearance. This SWM expresses no interest in character or marriage. He also seems to be overeager to impress (his yacht, his medical specialty.) Norma's radar clearly detects a "seduction scenario". As she is tired of fending these off, she decides that this is a definite "move on".

## *Zeroing In*

You now know what qualities you should look for. Here are some of the *key self-description words:* sincere, family-oriented, responsible, caring, warm. Always look for these clusters or traits.

Here are some of the *key goal words:* friendship, permanent relationship, commitment, marriage. Any ads that don't radiate these signals may be appropriate for other people, but not for a serious mate-seeker like yourself.

There are also some "signalling" words used in the context of singles communications which sometimes differ from the dictionary definitions. Some of these differences are amusing, some dangerous. Keep alert for the following nuances, so you won't be misled.

### Glossary of "Pay Attention!" Words

SENSUAL = interested in making speedy sexual contact, possibly not much else
ROMANTIC = same as sensual
AFFECTIONATE = same as sensual
GENEROUS = same as sensual
EASY-GOING = same as sensual
BIG HEARTED = same as sensual

PASSIONATE = same as sensual
BROADMINDED = same as sensual
FRIENDLY = same as sensual
INFLAMMABLE (also IGNITABLE) = wants to be sensual—
    you do the work
CUDDLY = seeking replacement for teddy bear
KNOWS HOW TO PLEASE A MAN/WOMAN = desperate
S & M = wishes to engage in sado-masochistic sex activities
BI = bisexual, may be interested in involving you in a trio, may have
    AIDS
REFINED (men) = promises not to attack you sexually right away
REFINED (women) = doesn't want to be approached sexually right
    away, maybe never
SHY = a clam (see refined)
QUIET = same as shy
HOMEBODY = a zombie; or seeking a home (yours); sometimes
    both
STRAPPING LAD = either overweight, into S & M, or both
GENEROUSLY PROPORTIONED = fat
ZAFTIG = a fat lady
GREAT BODY = no mind
SEEKING PLATONIC FRIEND = uninterested in sex, scared of
    sex, or unable
DEVOUT CHRISTIAN = uninterested in sex (sometimes: just a
    churchgoer)
SEPARATED or SEP. = married (usually)—be suspicious
DIVORCE IN PROGRESS = same as separated
MAN (or WOMAN) IN TRANSITION = sometimes means
    divorce in progress, unemployed, having a mental
    breakdown, or all three
GOOD SENSE OF HUMOR = can be anything from merely witty
    to clownish, infantile, unreliable, obnoxious
OPEN TO ADVENTURE = swinger
SEEKING SECURE RELATIONSHIP = chiefly interested in
    money (yours)
HAVE INDEPENDENT INCOME = and it's mine, all mine

A LOT TO LOVE = grossly overweight

WELL-ENDOWED = conceited, possibly pudgy, or has had silicone injections

UNPREJUDICED = desperate

LOOKS 50 = only if you need glasses

COMPANIONABLE = looking for a place to live (yours)

EASY TO GET ALONG WITH = if you're willing to be a doormat

UNENCUMBERED = a rolling stone

LAID BACK = too pooped to pop

PARTY ANIMAL = a lush

NIGHT OWL = either a lush or Dracula

A LIVE WIRE = frantic

ENJOYS KEEPING BUSY = a workaholic, has time to see you on alternate Tuesday evenings in July

HAVE SPARE ROOM FOR VISITING GUESTS = door does not lock

RELOCATABLE = unemployed, needs a place to live (yours)

RESEMBLES (name of movie star) = a jerk by any name

CRAZY ABOUT DANCING = can't talk, doesn't read

AUDIO BUFF = will listen to anything, except you

STRONG, SILENT TYPE = a potted plant

MOODY = I throw things, especially when I'm drunk

YOUTHFUL = older than he or she is admitting

## Liars of Both Sexes—How to Protect Yourself

What about lies? It is occasionally true that a crafty Don Juan or his scheming female counterpart Dona Juanita may have also mastered the "right" vocabulary. The personal ad or singles club three-line self-description would then be a complete misrepresentation. Recognizing that there may be a few skillful imposters out there, how do you spot them?

The next section, on answering ads and eliciting further information, provides you with the "safety equipment" and additional selection-making guidelines you need. You're about to make contact!

## *Your Next Step:* *Closing the Gap*

If you've decided that someone sounds interesting enough from his or her brief self-description to make contacting that person worthwhile, you now need a cover letter to enclose with your profile.

You don't have to be the soul of wit to write an effective cover letter. Once you have finished the decoding, discriminating, and decision-making process, contacting a mate-prospect is fairly simple.

## *Cover Letters that Get Results*

You need only two or three items to enclose in the envelope you're addressing to the person who intrigued you:
1. Your own profile or resumé (keep a large supply of these on hand).
2. A brief cover letter to attach.
3. (Optional) A clear, recent photograph of yourself to exchange, if you want to do that. However, many people, especially women, do not like the idea of circulating their photos through the mail in case they fall into the wrong hands. Only you can decide whether or not it's to your advantage to include the photo and request the other party's.

The cover letter, then, is the only essential item you don't have ready to go. We suggest you write a short, friendly, open-ended note following this model:

"Hi!

I saw your ad in the _____ Magazine (or read your Single _____ lovers profile) and I was so favorably impressed that I couldn't resist contacting you. You sound like just the kind of person I would like to get to know. As you will see from my enclosed profile, I share many of your interests and we seem to value similar personality traits. If you think, as I do, that it might be fun for us to meet, just drop me a line at P.O. Box 97 or call me at 212-555-1212 after 6 p.m. so we can set a time and place.

Hope to see you soon . . .''

That's all there is to it! Keep a large supply of these standard cover letters on hand and adapt them appropriately to individual cases. Then clip the letter to your profile, find an envelope and stamp, and you're all set. Get ready for a *very* interesting phone call or mail delivery.

*What if you get no answer?* Assume that the advertiser is too busy or, for whatever reason, changed his/her mind about meeting people since placing the ad. *Never* assume that you have failed to arouse interest—you have plenty to offer and there are lots of active people who *will* be beating a path to your mailbox or answering machine in short order. Always remember the basic guiding principle: you only have to find *one* Mr. or Ms. Right. Persevere!

Let's take the more likely outcome of your answering a few promising ads or descriptions. *What do you do with all the possibilities?* Now you're approaching the moment of deciding whether or not to make face-to-face contact and, if yes, how to manage it best. How do you handle this step of the selection process? The next chapter, CLOSE ENCOUNTERS: HOW TO TELL THE WINNERS FROM THE LOSERS, shows you what to do.

# Chapter Six

## CLOSE ENCOUNTERS: HOW TO TELL THE WINNERS FROM THE LOSERS

### *Information, Please!*

Once you start your program for meeting members of the opposite sex by any one of a variety of organized methods, the first step is always to get *information*—from such sources as profiles, singles news bulletins, letters, periodical "personal" ads, videotapes or recorded telephone announcements.

This chapter will reveal how to tell prospective "winning" dates from prospective "losing" dates. It will help you find someone worthwhile, save you from wasting a lot of time, and show you how to avoid unpleasant experiences.

First of all, let's assume that a particular "personal" ad or brief three-line mention in a singles letter has caught your eye. Here, you think, is someone worth investigating further.

You have either written a short letter asking for more information or you have sent away for the person's profile.

Here's what happens:

## Roseanne Doesn't Want to be a Sex-Toy

Harry sounded good to Roseanne, so she obtained his profile. Now she finds that Harry claims to be a mechanical engineer, long-divorced, prefers shapely redheads, and likes country & western music. But she's a young widow who teaches school for a living. Is Harry right for her? Probably not. The long timespan since his divorce indicates he might be a "swinger," and his lack of description of personality traits in a desirable date indicates that he either doesn't know what he wants, or else he considers women to be merely sex-objects or toys. His technical work indicates that he may not be very people-oriented. His taste in music clashes violently with hers.

George, on the other hand, has a much more intriguing profile sheet. He's been divorced long enough, two years or so, to get over the shock of the breakup, but not long enough to want to keep playing the field permanently.

George indicates that he likes women who are "sensitive and level-headed." He belongs to several clubs, and says he values "friends, children, and pets." He likes classical music and soft rock. His values and tastes seem to coincide closely with Roseanne's.

Roseanne drops him a note with a copy of her own profile, and suggests they meet in some safe, public place: a coffeeshop or a restaurant. They talk, and she finds that he seems to be very much like his "profile" sheet. A few more dates and they may be embarked on a romance with great possibilities for both.

## Andrew Decides Ballet and Bowling Don't Mix

Andrew, a lawyer with varied cultural interests, views a videotape of Lucille. In her interview, she presents herself as attractive and well-dressed. However, when he reads Lucille's profile, he discovers that aside from her secretarial job, she seems to have no interests except bowling and needlework. Since Andrew likes companions for ballet and opera, and hates sports, he quickly determines that it would be a waste of time to contact Lucille, and tells the videotape interviewer that he's just not interested.

But when he sees Cathy's videotape, he's delighted. She appears lively and enthusiastic about cultural activities. He tells the interviewer that he'd like to meet her, and she tells the interviewer that it is OK for Andrew to call her. Andrew asks her to go to the ballet with him, and she accepts with pleasure. Both approach their meeting with eager anticipation.

## Roger Avoids "Shrinking Violet"

Roger, an accountant, reads Joan's "personal" in the local paper. It says she's blond, shy, deeply religious, age 39, never married, and wonders why she's never been married. He reads the danger signals correctly, and decides not to answer the ad.

Another ad catches his eye. It says the woman is an "independent lady", with an established career, who likes outdoor sports and wants to meet a respectable male, mid-30's, for possible commitment.

Roger is intrigued enough to reply, and soon hears from Sherry. They seem to have much in common, particularly a fondness for cross-country skiing. They agree to go skiing together, and have a very promising exchange of ideas on physical fitness, winter sports, resorts, and a lot of other things. A beautiful friendship begins.

## Red Flags to Watch For

Once again, the guiding principle for taking a first, second and third step in beginning a relationship is "Know Thyself." Be honest with yourself about what you really like and want, and you'll have little trouble in deciding what to look for in an acquaintance of the opposite sex.

To avoid getting burned, however, there are certain "red flags"— danger signals you should watch for.

One is the obvious lie. If, for example, a man says he is "well-built" and turns out to weigh 400 pounds when you meet him, this is a clear indication to have a brief cup of coffee, unpack your "parachute" (your pre-planned polite excuse for leaving early), and depart. Needless to say, any further offers of dates are declined.

Similarly, if a woman claims her age is 40 and encloses a long-distance snapshot of somewhat fuzzy quality, be suspicious. And, if you do meet her and discover the photo must have been taken 10 or more years ago, that's your signal to buy her an inexpensive drink and suddenly remember you have to attend an important business meeting. On the other hand, if she keeps calling you, tell her tactfully you don't feel that your interests are compatible. If you feel uncomfortable with the truth—tell her you are seeing someone else (and do so).

In short, if you spot an obvious lie, beat a hasty retreat. Look elsewhere: the number of compatible, single members of the opposite sex is much larger than most people expect. Be selective. There are plenty of nice ones out there.

### Translating the Language of Love: Getting Acquainted

Some lies, however, are not so obvious. But if you listen carefully to what the other person is saying, some of these "red flags" may pop up:

"Free-lance" as an occupation usually means unemployed (there are some clear exceptions to this, but don't do anything hasty before you see some proof).

"I need my space" usually means "I want no commitments. I travel a lot and I'm generally unreliable." You definitely don't need a "drop-in/drop-out" relationship.

An interest you don't share—particularly *solitary hobbies* such as stamp-collecting, tropical fish, or ham radio, usually means that the person prefers to be alone. This sort of person usually turns out to be a boring, untalkative date—and usually can't stand you, either.

A person who emphasizes that he or she needs "patience and understanding" is really telling you "I want someone to help me grow up"—which may not be exactly what you had in mind. (It usually turns out to be very unrewarding if the person is over 21).

46

"Almost divorced" or "divorce in progress" may mean that the person is still living with a spouse. Or the "almost divorced" one may be just a married swinger. Don't do anything rash until you check this situation out *very* carefully.

Watch out for a guy or gal from a far-away area who would like to see you on a "business trip." A lot of these people are legitimate—but a lot of them have at least one spouse somewhere else. It's best to avoid this type—for reasons of health, if nothing else. They can play havoc with your emotional well-being, too.

## Age-Fixations, Mental Zeroes, Zombies, and Other Bad News

Another "red flag" to watch out for is the person whose stated preference in age is more than ten years over or under the age they say they are. Some of these people have psychological kinks you may not want to contend with. (Of course, if this sort of thing turns you on, there's no shortage of willing partners, but we don't recommend it.)

You definitely should determine whether or not the other person is "dead from the neck up" or a mental zero. If your dates ever indicate that they've read no contemporary books or seen any recent movies, their mental growth may have stopped years ago. Such people are "back-dated," and can be incredibly boring after you get to know them.

However, you may want to give them a chance. Sometimes life can get unavoidably hectic for some people and they just don't have the opportunity to keep up with things. Perhaps your mental stimulation will be welcomed. Try a few "test dates" to see if you can stir up any interest in things.

But remember, someone who has ceased to develop as a personality is a social zombie. You *can* do better. There are millions of constantly developing, self-improving single adults who would love to share some time—perhaps an evening or even a life—with you.

Then there are the gays. You probably won't run into them in the normal course of events, but they do turn up occasionally. Some are bi-sexuals. Some are trying to become "straight." And others may just have been confused and filled out the wrong form (yes, there are dating organizations for homosexuals, too). Many of them are nice people, but—unless you're filled with crusading zeal and think you can change their basic orientation (the success rate is very low)—you should bow out of the situation gracefully.

## Mama's Boys and Late Bloomers

What about the person over 40 who has never been married? With some exceptions, this type of personal history indicates a lack of sustained interest in the opposite sex, or a lack of ability to be perceived as interesting by any member of it. A note of caution: there are a few, acceptable "late bloomers" in this category who shouldn't be overlooked. But even they are usually pretty set in their ways by 40, and have a lot of trouble making an adjustment to living with another person.

People over 25 who are still living with one or both of their parents are also suspect. By modern American standards, this situation is abnormal. It indicates a clear dating handicap and also may reveal psychological hang-ups about growing up and forming adult attachments.

Here's what can happen:

Mary agreed to go out with Howard, age 45, a computer expert whose profile showed he had never been married and lived with his widowed mother. Mary thought there might be a chance to establish a relationship, because they had a mutual interest in computer games.

Alas, instead of taking her to a restaurant, a movie, or even a video game arcade, Howard solemnly brought her home to Momma. Tedious conversation ensued, all about Momma's early life, her relatives, her pets past and present, and her aches and pains. Mary got the message. She concluded that Howard was not for her.

## Red Flags on the Phone

There are "red flags" in telephone introductions, too—just as there are in ads, profiles, letters, and face-to-face encounters. Some of these are: extreme speech defects, stuttering to the point of unintelligibility, mumbling, and sometimes hardness of hearing.

A really bad sign is immediate "sex talk" of the obscene phone-call variety. These people often turn out to be dangerous in person. Just hang up the phone, and if they persist, call the police. You can also get the phone company to change your number. *Make sure you get an unlisted one*, so people can't look up your address in the phone book and come by in person. Fortunately, such experiences are quite rare.

Less obvious "red flags" include the sound of a loud sportscast or soap opera in the background—unless you, too, like that sort of thing. Long silences between sentences may indicate either great nervousness or chronic blankness of mind.

Great caution in talking about oneself may indicate the presence of a spouse (!) or perhaps just curious children, nosy roommates, or nearby co-workers.

A relatively brief conversation (under 10 minutes) should establish whether you and your caller have any common ground that would make it worth your while to agree to a face-to-face meeting. It also demonstrates that time is valuable to both of you.

However, if your caller can't schedule a cup of coffee with you until the third Thursday of next month, it may indicate that either he or she is a "workaholic" or is all dated up—neither situation being very promising for a long-term relationship.

If you're contacting a custodial parent (a mother or father with small kids around), be prepared for the noise of children in the background. If this bothers you, you should look elsewhere—there are plenty of singles with no kids, or with grown ones who live apart.

On the other hand, if the person you're talking to sounds very anti-children, you might conclude you're talking to a solitary, crabby Scrooge or old-maid type of person—possibly alcoholic—and cut the conversation short.

People who talk exclusively about themselves or the problems of their job or business are not good bets either, unless you like being ignored. They won't mind if you hang up. They like talking to themselves better than anyone else, anyway.

Callers who persist in trying to date you after being dropped are either dense or desperate. You may have to resort to rudeness. Don't let it bother you. They're used to it.

But be of good cheer. For every one of the losers we've warned you about, there are many desirable people anxious to meet you.

## Turn-Off Signs at a First Meeting

"Turn-Off" signs at a first meeting are usually easier to spot than "red flags" in profiles and phone calls. They include extreme lateness, obvious intoxication, lipstick smears, nasty behavior to restaurant personnel, inappropriate dress for the place selected, lack of conversation, or conversation only on boring or narcissistic subjects, and obvious differences in person from the profile or telephone self-description.

For example, someone claiming to be a teacher should be regarded with suspicion if he talks like a hillbilly.

Other "turn-off" signals include visible bad habits, such as severe nailbiting, chain-smoking, and serious over-eating. There can be many others, depending on your individual tastes and standards.

"Turn-on" behavior at a first meeting, on the other hand, can be equally clear. It is usually the reverse of the "turn off" or "forget it" signals—general consideration toward you, warmth, active common interests, free self-disclosure—in short, being true to or even exceeding the expectations which preceded the first meeting. When you experience this kind of behavior, relax and enjoy what may be the beginning of a beautiful friendship.

## What Happens Next?

Now that you have, we hope, taken the first steps toward finding your romance, go on to Chapter Seven, WE MEET AGAIN: FILLING OUT THE PICTURE, for guidelines on the second and third dates.

# Chapter Seven

## WE MEET AGAIN: FILLING OUT THE PICTURE

### I. THE THREE R's: RE-CONTACTING, REFLECTING, RATING

*Re-Contacting and How to Do It*

You have now met someone who may turn out to be very special. You've had a pleasant dinner together and now you want to meet again. How do you follow up?

First of all, you want to make that second contact as *promptly* as possible. Consider this common dilemma that Hector and Shirley found themselves facing after their first date:

Hector had been thrilled to meet Shirley, a lively and witty young woman of the type he most admired. They had talked in the restaurant until the waiter reminded them it was closing time. Then, only after Hector had hailed her a taxi in the rain and cheerily waved her off, did he remember that in the rush to pay the check he hadn't set a specific time for their next date. Hector cursed himself and wondered what to do. Should he wait a "decent interval," like a Victorian suitor, before calling her again? Hector felt that delay would be frustrating to him and confuse Shirley. He resolved to call her the very next evening.

Shirley, riding away in the taxi, also realized that Hector hadn't set a time for their next meeting. She knew that he wanted to see her again. Should she wait passively, "all alone by the telephone"? Shirley resolved to trust her answering machine and go on with her life as usual, including a date with another man scheduled for the next evening. Meanwhile, though, she dropped Hector a friendly, humorous post card thanking him for a memorable dinner.

What happened? When Shirley returned home the next evening, discouraged after a date of the "b & b" variety (brief and boring), she found Hector's pleasant voice on the machine suggesting a time and place. Shirley was delighted. She would return his call the following day.

Meanwhile, Hector received Shirley's postcard. He was pleased that he had made such a favorable impression and more eager than ever to see Shirley again. When Shirley returned Hector's call before he had finished reading the day's mail, they both laughed over the delay and its happy resolution.

What is the moral of their re-connection story? *Passivity is out—take action!* Excessively slow, constrained, Victorian-era dating behavior on the part of *either* sex is regarded nowadays as lacking in warmth, spontaneity, and consideration. Neither Hector nor Shirley "came on too strong." They simply expressed enthusiasm. If you are interested, it's appropriate to show it. Take the risk; make that follow-up phone call promptly, send that postcard.

What if you have a fabulous first date and neither party follows up? Again, don't wait and hope. Simply assume that he or she had too many other irons in the fire and you are well out of a potential relationship with a charmer who leads a date on just for fun. In this case, you've saved a lot of valuable time. Take steps to meet someone else as soon as possible—someone better.

### *Reflecting: Detecting Hidden Clues to Personality*

While you are waiting for your second date to take place, you could be busy reviewing that exciting first date in emotional tranquility. Try to capture the overall "feeling-tone" of the experience, just as recording engineers set room-tone sound tracks to capture the subtle background noises of a particular space. Sort out the "vibes" that you felt. In the course of Shirley's reflections on her dinner with Hector, for example, she consciously noticed something significant that she had only glimpsed out of the corner of her eye before—that Hector had been very nervous. He had obviously enjoyed their meeting but had fidgeted and perspired a good deal. Was Hector worried about a problem at the office? Was he especially anxious to impress her? Or was he a tense, high-strung person? Shirley made a mental note to observe if he was still nervous on their second date and, if so, to ask him about it tactfully.

When Hector first saw Shirley, he noticed merely that she had a pretty face and a nice figure. Upon reflection on her appearance, it occurred to him that Shirley had clearly paid exquisite attention to every detail of grooming. Her manicure was perfect, not a hair was out of place, her antique gold brooch beautifully complemented her elegant suit. Hector wondered: Was it just that Shirley had high standards and excellent taste in matters of appearance? Had she made an unusual effort that evening to impress him? Or was she perhaps a "neat freak"? Hector made a mental note to observe if she was still groomed to cover-girl perfection on their next date and, if so, to probe gently.

In their private reflections, both Hector and Shirley were registering for the first time all the important little clues to personality they had missed in the excitement of the first meeting. They were, in effect, replaying their mental videotapes of that evening at a slower speed in order to become more aware of significant details. This active kind of recollection could be regarded as "homework" or preparation for the next date.

### *Rating: The Contrast Method of Evaluation*

Think about the circumstances of your first meeting with a person who later became your best friend or worst enemy. Now that you know that individual thoroughly, couldn't you have predicted from the interactions of your first meeting what kind of personality would emerge over time? Most people think so. Their stories usually begin, "I should have know when . . ." and lead up to whatever ending the relationship had.

For example, on her first date with her last boyfriend Pete, Shirley recalled that he was late in arriving, offered no excuses, bullied the restaurant manager for not holding his reservation longer, and flustered the waitress by changing his order three times. Later on in their short relationship Shirley discovered that Pete's behavior that night was consistent with his overall character—he turned out to be a highly disorganized, inconsiderate person. Shirley now wants to make sure that she is alert to personality possibilities much earlier on.

On her first date with Hector, Shirley was especially pleased that he was punctual and courteous. She liked it a lot when he left a generous tip and apologized personally to the waiter for failing to notice that it was near closing time. In making a tentative evaluation of Hector, Shirley therefore rates him very highly.

Hector could also tell a story beginning, "I should have known better when . . ." in relation to his previous girlfriend Dora. On their first date, a New Year's Eve party given by the local political club, Dora talked non-stop to Hector and any other pair of ears that would listen. She didn't wait for responses before jabbering on. Her conversation revolved around herself, her apartment, her job, her plants. Instead of drawing the correct conclusion, that Dora was a rather dizzy and self-centered person, Hector continued to date for some weeks in an increasingly puzzled, dispirited fashion, hoping to break through the wall of words. When his efforts failed, Hector withdrew, determined never to overlook such clear "early warning signals" again.

On his first date with Shirley, Hector was especially pleased she could carry on a sensible, interesting conversation. She communicated openly about herself but also asked Hector about himself and genuinely listened when he replied. Shirley spoke in thoughtful, complete sentences. Hector particularly liked the way Shirley would pause for a moment to find a word with the exact nuance of meaning she wanted to convey. He speculated that her conversational style might reflect a logical, well-organized mind and a stable personality. In making a tentative evaluation of Shirley, Hector therefore rates her highly.

You have now mastered the three R's—re-contacting, reflecting, and rating. You are almost ready to conclude these fruitful armchair meditations and dress for your second date.

### When A Brush-Off Is Really a Come-On, Don't Proceed

Phyllis experienced a bit of confusion as she reflected on her date with Ben. Ben seemed to enjoy her company and they shared many interests, yet he was a little cool at parting. He had sighed wistfully as he said good night, whispering, "You're almost right, but—"

Is this a brush-off? Phyllis wondered. Analyzing Ben's behavior more closely, she determined that he was instead giving her a common kind of come-on. Ben wanted her to pursue *him*, to wear herself out showing him that she was "really right," not just "almost right."

Phyllis did not rise to this stale bait. Thanks to her period of reflection, she identified Ben's ploy correctly and crossed him off her list.

Remember: *you don't have to prove yourself.* If your date tries to tease you into a head-game of this kind, just say "Pass" to any further contact and move on to someone more worthy of your time.

## II. INTERMEDIATE "GETTING-TO-KNOW-YOU" DATES

### The Second Date: Choosing a Place

The ideal setting for a second date should be fairly private, non-stressful, and quiet. Walk the trail around the lake in a nearby state park, for example, or take a picnic to the beach. If it's winter or raining, stroll through a less-frequented wing of a museum.

Avoid noises, crowds, and distractions. Your purpose when you meet again, after all, is to talk, to get to know each other better. Remember that you are still engaged in the interviewing sequence of your search for a life-partner. You are not interested in entertainment at this point but in *exploration.* You are both exploring each other's potential as mates. You have made only one commitment so far: time. On the second date, you should allot more time than you did for the first meeting and it should be uninterrupted time. Get far away from ringing hones, eavesdropping waiters, or any other intrusions. You can be near people, if it makes you feel more comfortable, but not in the midst of them.

Let's say you and your date consider the possibilities and agree to spend a relaxing afternoon strolling along the seashore. Already you know more about each other than you did before—you are both capable of enjoying casual, unstructured activities in the outdoors. Now let's follow five couples through their Saturday at the beach.

## The Second Date Is the Life-History Date

The second date usually determines whether or not you want to develop the relationship or end it. It is during this longer stretch of time that people usually exchange life-histories in greater detail than their first meeting permitted. These more revealing exchanges are usually decisive, so listen up!

## Colleen Feels Swamped by Sy, the Psycho-Babbler

When Colleen first met Sy for a coffee-date after the "Save the Whales" demonstration in which they were both participating, she was pleased when he confided that he was in psychotherapy. At last, she remembered thinking, a man with insight, a man who can admit it when he needs help, a man who actually wants to grow up. It was all very refreshing.

Colleen didn't have to wait long for Sy to tell her more about his therapy or, to be precise, therapies. Sy had been involved in primal scream therapy, Jungian, Adlerian, bio-energetics, art therapy, Esalen, Rolfing, and every other form of therapy Colleen had ever heard of (and some she had not). He had been in all these therapies for brief periods of time as he flitted from California to Maine, from job to job.

Moreover, Sy spoke a peculiar jargon. He couldn't relate an event; he had to "share an experience." He didn't socialize much; he "needed his space" in order to "get in touch with his feelings," to find out "where his head was at."

By this point in the afternoon, Colleen found her eyes wandering away repeatedly to the seagulls over the waves, then back to her wristwatch. She decided to interrupt Sy's "flow" (which didn't faze him a bit) by suggesting they return earlier due to her sunburn. Fortunately, Sy hadn't noticed her applying sun-block lotion when they arrived, so he agreed. He bade Colleen a fond farewell as he departed for an extra hour in his sensory-deprivation tank, complimenting her that she was "such a good listener." Colleen breathed a sigh of relief and hurried home to call a friend. She could dine out on Sy-jokes for weeks to come.

What did Colleen lose? Only a few hours of her time. What did she gain? A little useful, harmless experience (and a wealth of "California flake" comedy material). What did she keep throughout? *Her options.* She was able to spot Sy as an unsuitable mate-prospect early on, thus freeing herself for better opportunities.

## Clark Can't Get a Straight Answer Out of Trite Terry

When Clark first met Terry, a public relations executive, he had been impressed with her effortless charm and easy flow of speech. He remembered comparing her in his mind with his ex-wife, one of the leading Slow Talkers of America. What a pleasant surprise, Clark had thought—a woman who can express herself! On their second date, Clark asked Terry a few questions about her previous marriage and settled back to hear what this fluent lady would have to say.

Terry smiled fetchingly at Clark and proceeded to comment on her recently-ended, seven-year marriage. Her account featured such unilluminating statements as, "Gee, I don't know—I guess we just drifted apart," "We went our separate ways," "We just didn't seem to have much in common anymore," and "It was just one of those things."

Puzzled by her vagueness on this important topic, Clark decided to ask a more specific questions—why Terry and her ex-husband never had children. When she answered, "Gee, I guess we didn't discuss it much," Clark fell silent, stumped. Then he mustered his energies for one last, irresistible question. "In seven years?" he asked incredulously.

Terry ceased smiling. "Let's say the topic didn't come up often," she said firmly, and added: "What are you, nosy?"

Clark apologized to Terry and said he was sorry if he had intruded on her privacy, but in his mind he decided that the date was over as soon as he could decently end it. Clark knew that he had a right and a legitimate need to question a mate-prospect about her past relationships and to invite questions in return about his. He correctly regarded marriage as a very serious undertaking and the ending of it as a painful, important, revealing decision. he collection of cliches Terry emitted offered Clark no insight into her former marriage. Her glibness did, however, provide him with some useful information about Terry. Either she was concealing some embarrassing truth about herself or, more likely, she was simply a shallow, non-introspective woman.

Clark had been forced to do a lot of thinking since the jolt of his divorce and in the course of talking to divorced friends and dates. He had come to the conclusion that a person who had developed no insight from such a major life-upheaval as a divorce was like a person driving a car without a license—very, very dangerous. Clark therefore resolved to jump out of the path of Trite Terry. He began cleaning up their picnic site and pointed out some approaching rain clouds. Terry took the hint graciously, relieved to be off the hook.

What did Clark lose? Only a few hours' time. What did Clark learn? A little healthy suspicion of glib talkers. What did Clark gain? Safety and the option of exploring other, better mate-prospects.

Clark went home cheerfully, looking forward to contacting several other ladies whose profiles he had collected. It was going to be a busy week.

### Janet Discovers Her Date is a "Deadbeat Dad"

When Janet first met Vic for a cocktail after work, she had been impressed by his mentioning that he had recently acquired a season's box at the city opera. She remembered thinking to herself: At last! A cultured man! But during a second date at the beach, Janet began to have misgivings. Vic had hailed her in the parking lot by braking his new Porsche to a screeching halt and calling out, "Like it? It's an advance present to myself. I'm expecting a great divorce settlement!"

Janet began to suspect that the opera tickets had originally belonged to Vic's wife. She resolved to ask Vic some leading questions about his divorce-in-progress.

Vic was anxious to discuss his litigation in detail. "I have the perfect divorce strategy," he bragged.

From Janet's point of view as an experienced paralegal, Vic's "strategy" turned out to be nothing more than a form of legalized blackmail. He and his lawyer were in the process of suing for custody of the two children on the trumped-up ground that Vic's wife Charlotte was a "morally unfit" mother. With only a little prompting from Janet, the real facts of the case emerged.

Charlotte had wanted to end the marriage for several years upon discovering Vic's affair with a receptionist ("Imagine that!" Vic had exclaimed indignantly. "Just for a brief affair!") When Vic refused to leave the family home, Charlotte was at wits' end. When she began proceedings to obtain a court order for his eviction, Vic finally cooperated, although only after she had agreed to let him take a substantial amount of money from their joint account for a posh apartment.

Before their separation papers were completed, Charlotte had imprudently invited a male friend over for dinner with her and the children. The man hadn't actually stayed the night but, as Vic boasted proudly, "I have buddies I can count on to lie for me in court."

Offended by Vic's unscrupulous treatment of Charlotte and vindictive misuse of the judicial system, Janet asked him what he would do with the children if he managed to win custody. Vic revealed his plan to send them to boarding school in the winter and "park" them with his retired parents in the summer.

When Janet asked Vic if he was finding interim support payments a financial strain while his costly legal maneuverings dragged the divorce case into its third year, he explained that he had twice moved to dodge prosecution for failure to provide court-ordered child support.

Janet became increasingly disgusted at Vic's unwarranted, unethical, and sometimes illegal persecution of Charlotte through the courts.

Clearly, he had not ended the relationship emotionally. He had no insight into his contribution to the break-up, accepted no proper responsibility, and continued to punish Charlotte by attempting to blacken her reputation and deprive both mother and children of a stable relationship with each other. Worst of all, Vic's disregard for the psychological and financial well-being of his children, presumably the most important attachments in a parent's life, revealed a profoundly immature character.

Janet became aware that she had been staring at the waves for some time as she listened to Vic. Finally, she asked him if he thought his legal manipulations were hurting his children. At this question, Vic was highly incensed. "What do you mean? Whose side are you on, anyway?" he asked.

Vic proceeded to tear out from his bulging wallet the many profiles he had received from women contacting him first. He waved them under Janet's nose.

"You're lucky you made the first round!" Vic snorted.

Janet picked up her picnic basket. "You didn't," she said and left.

As Janet strode back to her car alone, she resolved never again to make the mistake of granting a Vengeful Vic a second date. But her brief "disaster date" with Vic had produced the beneficial side-effect of intensifying her motivation to be more selective, starting with step one. Reminder: What do you do with turkeys? *Stuff thetm!*

## The Etiquette of Endings: Graceful Good-byes

You don't have to be impolite about ending a relationship unwisely begun, as Janet was with Vic, but you do owe it to yourself to be speedy—your time is valuable. Move on to spending it with a more rewarding partner. Try to be kind and tactful with your good-byes, as Colleen and Clark were in the circumstances of their disappointing second dates—but don't dally. Prolonging it falsely encourages your date while wasting your time. You don't want to do either.

## Spencer Tunes Out Millie the Martyr

When Spencer first met Millie, he had been impressed by her apparent domesticity. She enjoyed decorating her apartment and sewed most of her own clothes. Never married, Millie had expressed a strong interest in starting a home and having a family with the right fellow. Spencer, a pleasant young businessman who had been looking in vain for a nice homebody-type woman for over a year, began to feel the stirrings of hope. When they were strolling on the beach, Spencer asked Millie what she had been doing during the week that had passed since their last meeting.

Instead of a reply, Spencer heard a long list of complaints. Millie's auto mechanic had, she suspected, failed to repair her car properly—it was still stalling. He had over-charged her, too, she was sure. Then Millie's dry cleaners told her they couldn't remove a grass stain from her skirt and she was furious with their incompetence. After that, Millie's cat got sick and had to be taken to the vet. "Twenty dollars for a few pills!" Millie sniffed. "I bet they won't even work!"

Millie rattled on about untrustworthy washer repairmen, a taxi driver who had "deliberately" taken the longest route to her destination, and so on—and on. Spencer listened wearily. Millie, he concluded, was a professional martyr, a *kvetch* (a chronic complainer). The theme of her week's events was clearly "I've been cheated," even when she hadn't been. Millie saw herself as an innocent victim of malevolent forces.

Would Spencer enjoy hearing her recital of woes for the rest of his life? he asked himself. Worse, how would he like to be expected to fight Millie's endless little battles for her? The prospect appalled him.

In this case, Spencer appropriately decided to skip the life-history questions. One week of Millie's experiences had provided him with more than enough data to conclude that they were definitely not compatible.

Spencer decided to tune out, murmur "uh-huh" at suitable intervals, relax, and work on his tan until it drew near time to go home. It was at least restful at the beach and Spencer had some thinking to do about the profiles he had left on his desk. The women who had described themselves as "cheerful and self-reliant" were beginning to look better and better.

## Love at Second Sight: Ron and Ingrid Meet Again

Ron and Ingrid already knew a lot about each other. On their first date, they had found themselves discussing the important people in their daily lives, their family, friends, and co-workers. In fact, as Ron and Ingrid discovered in later periods of solitary reflection, it seemed they were both highly people-oriented. Their lives were populated with a stable cast of "significant others," including one dog each "who thinks he's a person."

Today their date at the beach had an inauspicious beginning which produced an unexpectedly marvelous result. Ron was already waiting in the parking lot when Ingrid drove up slowly, nursing a half-deflated tire. She got out, greeted Ron, and kicked the tire. "Sorry if I'm a little late," she said. "Amazing Grace here got cantankerous."

Ron laughed at the car's name and patted Ingrid's dachshund. "No problem," he said, lifting a jack out of the trunk of his car. "Where's your spare tire?"

Pleasantly surprised by Ron's readiness to help, Ingrid thought for a moment whether she should accept his offer or suggest calling her road service as usual. Ron sensed her polite hesitation and added, "You could help, if you want to."

Ingrid promptly found the spare tire and asked Ron what to do. He spread out some tools. "You just hand me the lug wrench when I need it," he said, "and don't let the nuts roll under the car and get lost."

Soon Ron and Ingrid were absorbed in changing the tire, a process she had never observed closely before. They forgot any initial awkwardness. It began to be fun, just working together in the sun. Ingrid smiled and thanked Ron for the tire-changing lesson. "I like to learn new things," she said. Ingrid began to tell Ron about the evening course in American literature she had taken last spring.

Ron was pleased. It happend that he had just signed up for an evening course in Chinese cooking. "Even the dog was tired of my chili," he laughed.

As Ron and Ingrid unpacked the food that they had both brought, they were beginning to perceive each other positively as growing, flexible individuals. Ron particularly liked the fresh fruit salad Ingrid had prepared. "I've never tasted kiwi fruit before," he remarked. "It's delicious."

Ingrid enjoyed watching Ron build a fire with the charcoal he had remembered to bring. He seemed a very capable fellow.

Neither Ingrid nor Ron had ever grilled chicken breasts before, but together they gave it a try. Ron's barbecue sauce and Ingrid's dexterity with a cooking fork saved the meat from drying out. "We work well together," Ingrid observed. Ron agreed with enthusiasm.

As the afternoon drew lazily on, Ron and Ingrid sat together on the sand and talked a little about their pasts. Ron, age 27, confided frankly that he had ended his marriage two years ago because of irreconciliable sexual differences. His ex-wife Margaret, who had always been rather inhibited, withdrew from Ron sexually after the birth of their only child, his "darling daughter Donna." As Ron commented ruefully, "Margaret was a classic. She always 'had a headache'."

He had tried to interest her in marriage counseling but she insisted that there was nothing wrong with her—Ron just needed a hobby. As Ron already had several hobbies, he began to conclude painfully that divorce was essential for his well-being. He considered Margaret a competent mother but, for him, an inadequate life-partner. Moreover, Ron enjoyed fatherhood and Margaret had refused even to consider having another child. Finally, it was clear he had to move out.

In the case of the "rejects" Sy, Terry, Vic, and Millie, there was zero evidence in their life-histories of current, genuine personality development and little, if any, likelihood of constructive future changes (barring a major miracle). By contrast, the growth potential of Ron and Ingrid seems infinite. This creative couple could go on growing together as they have already proven they are able to do alone.

Meanwhile, Ron had been doing a fair amount of serious dating. He wanted to marry someone "alive and developing, without a lot of hang-ups." He also definitely desired more children. "I've got to have the experience of sharing a family with a woman I love," said Ron earnestly.

Ingrid longed for the same experience. A little younger than Ron, she had never been married and had no children. However, Ingrid confided she had recently ended a long-term relationship with a fellow who had been her supervisor while she was completing the student—teaching component of her Master's degree in science education. They had had a fairly stable, though tepid relationship for two years and everyone expected them to marry eventually. Ingrid had her reservations, though, especially when it became clear that Curtis was quite negative on the subject of having children. She had thought for a while that he might "grow up" and become more receptive to the idea.

However, Curtis never did. Instead, he withdrew further from their life together by means of obsessive involvement with solitary hobbies. Curtis spent entire evenings painstakingly building model airplanes and flying them by remote-control devices in distant cow pastures. On week-ends when the weather was poor, Curtis worked on his tropical fish collection, designing aquariums and muttering to himself about neon tetras, guppies, kissing gouramis, and Siamese fighting fish. When he brought home a piranha, it was the last straw. Ingrid announced that she was packing her suitcase. Oblivious, Curtis continued to feed sliced steak to the piranha, swimming in splendid isolation in its own tank. "I'll leave you two alone," Ingrid had wisecracked and slammed the door.

"So here I am," she concluded.

Still laughing at the piranha story, Ron hastened to assure Ingrid that his hobbies were not of the solitary kind. He liked playing tennis with friends, taking his daughter fishing, bowling with the team from his social work agency, and taking classes in unfamiliar subjects.

"I do have one solitary hobby that I'm looking for someone to share," Ron ventured. "I like to build my own furniture—bookcases, end-tables, that sort of thing."

Ingrid was intrigued. In order to save money and because of the challenge, she had recently purchased a do-it-yourself kit for a bookcase. However, she had been stumped when she read the first direction, which instructed her to use a Phillips screwdriver. "How would I know what that is?" she asked, laughing at her ignorance. Ron brightened at this unexpected opportunity and promptly offered to help her build the bookcase the next Saturday. Ingrid accepted on one condition: that she could then return the favor by helping Ron build a bookcase for his apartment.

"Great!" he agreed. "As a matter of fact, Donna needs one for all the Dr. Seuss books she keeps at my place."

As Ron and Ingrid strolled back to the parking lot hand-in-hand, they were both looking forward to what seemed to be the beginning of a beautiful romance. Ron gave Ingrid a warm good-night peck on the cheek. As she drove off Ingrid thought: My, he certainly beats a kissing gourami!

## Second Date Round-Up

The parking lot at the beach is now deserted and all our five couples have gone home. What do the most conscientious mate-searchers Colleen, Clark, Janet, Spencer, Ron, and Ingrid all have in common?

They all listened for *themes* in their dates' histories, not just facts. Colleen was able to determine from Sy's account of leapfrogging from therapy to therapy that he was too unstable for her needs. Clark perceived from the verbal evasions of Terry that she had no insight into the causes of her divorce and, consequently, that she could turn out to be harmful to others at close range. Janet was horrified to hear of Vic's gross disregard of his children's best interests. It took Spencer no time at all to conclude he was much better off "single but looking" than stuck with hearing Millie's chronic complaints for the rest of his life.

These seemingly unsuccessful second dates left a positive residue of useful information for future date-screening. In addition, the more discriminating parties on the dates returned home with the prospect of an endless supply of better mate-candidates waiting for them to make contact. All in all, it was an afternoon well-spent.

As for the successful couple, Ron and Ingrid, they too listened for *themes*. Ingrid thought that Ron was, above all, *responsible*—responsible to his own ideals for domestic happiness, responsible to his daughter, even responsible to a date he hardly knew (he had fixed her tire, brought the charcoal, and tended the campfire). His adult, manly pleasure in responsibility appealed to Ingrid enormously.

In Ron's musings about Ingrid, he was most impressed by what he perceived to be a pattern of *integrity* in her life. Ingrid had refused to compromise her normal desires for tender companionship and a marriage with children by leaving the boyfriend who could give her neither.

In their relatively brief relationship, Ron and Ingrid had already revealed another promising trait common to both: they liked to learn new things. They struck each other as lively, curious, adaptable, expanding personalities.

This character trait is perhaps the most important one to look for in a possible life-partner. Ask yourself: Is this person now a *growing* individual? What is the future *growth potential?*

In the case of the "rejects" Sy, Terry, Vic, and Millie, there was zero evidence in their life-histories of current, genuine personality development and little, if any, likelihood of constructive future changes (barring a major miracle). By contrast, the growth potential of Ron and Ingrid seems infinite. This creative couple could go on growing together as they have already proven they are able to do alone.

Ron and Ingrid also noticed that they were already fairly content in their single life-styles. Ron liked himself; Ingrid liked herself. They both yearned for greater fulfillment in a happy marriage but, meanwhile, they were active, sociable, and cheerful. Ron and Ingrid looked forward to marriage to increase their happiness, not to redeem them from emptiness. Remember: *A happy married person was once a happy single person.*

Some people you may meet are chronically unhappy. Millie the Martyr, for example, was wasting her life on whining and Vengeful Vic was wasting his in attempting to reduce others to his own level of misery. No one could make these "wasters" happy—they are unhappy with themselves.

Ron and Ingrid are clearly winners, not "wasters." Let's follow them into the next step of their interviewing sequence, the crucial third date.

## III. THE THIRD DATE IS THE PHILOSOPHY DATE

Like the refrain in a popular song, certain life-themes will re-appear if we listen to people attentively. Ron spotted integrity as one of Ingrid's leading characteristics, for example, and Ingrid noted responsibility as one of Ron's most promising traits.

On their third date, they will both be looking for confirmation or contradiction of their earlier impressions about each other's character. They have allowed for a longer period of time together, a Saturday afternoon plus the evening, and they have planned a quiet activity, building bookcases. By now Ingrid trusts Ron enough to invite him into her home for lunch and their joint carpentry efforts. Then she in turn will visit his home for dinner and more bookcase-building.

During their time together Ron and Ingrid will be conversing pleasantly about any topic that comes up. But no matter what the topic, they will be able to glean significant information about each other's values, priorities, and goals.

The third date is usually the one in which basic life-attitudes or philosophies emerge. These attitudes should be fairly compatible if the relationship is going to progress to marriage. For example, a person with a Golden Rule philosophy ("do unto others as you would have them do unto you") would be quite unhappy with a person whose approach to life was marked by a "dog-eat-dog" philosophy. Similarly, a Yuppie would not be happy with a hippie, nor a conservative Republican with a liberal Democrat, nor a strict Catholic with a militant atheist. Don't believe the cliche, "Opposites attract," for one second when it comes to philosophies. Compatibility of outlook is vital.

The professions of Ron, a social worker, and Ingrid, a high school teacher, already indicated strong, positive people-involvement. As Ron said, unpacking a screwdriver from his tool-box, he enjoyed feeling that his job was helping in even a small way to relieve human suffering and improve society. Ingrid understood. She derived pleasure from opening her students' eyes to a better understanding of the physical world and a better grasp of the technology they would need for success in their future lives.

As she passed Ron a shelf, Ingrid pointed ou that she and Ron seemed to share similar attitudes towards money. They had chosen professions in which no one ever got rich and here they were, economically building a bookcase instead of buying one ready-made. Ron laughed. "It's true," he said. "Personal satisfactions are more important to me than anything money can buy. Maybe that's why I like kids. God knows they're expensive to raise, but it's worth it."

Ingrid remarked that sharing a family with a man she could love had always been one of her chief goals. She enjoyed playing with her little nephew, but she wanted children of her own, too. To Ingrid, children were as much a priority as they were to Ron.

When they took a break for lunch, Ron noticed that Ingrid's apartment, though small, seemed well-organized and clutter-free. It gave him a peaceful feeling. "It's just like you," Ron observed appreciatively.

Later, when Ingrid was about to enter Ron's apartment, she steeled herself for a possible disappointment. She had seen the apartments of other divorced men and remembered picking her way among baskets of dirty laundry, stacks of books and magazines, and other bric-a-brac. What a delightful surprise when she entered Ron's apartment! Ingrid could walk among the comfortable articles of furniture without tripping over one cardboard box. "I was half-expecting a disaster area," Ingrid laughed. "This is a *home!*"

"A home is important to me, too," Ron replied. "Making a happy home with a wife and children is one of my chief objectives."

When they had finished building the second bookcase for Ron's little girl, Ingrid suggested they could add designs of baby animals with stencils from the school art room. Ron liked the idea and they went out to buy paint.

As they painted, and later as they lingered over Ron's simple but tasty Chinese dinner, the couple talked with animation about everything from politics to religious beliefs, from their involvement in caring for their aging parents to their current problems and challenges at work. In all the subjects they touched upon, one theme emerged time and time again: Ron and Ingrid valued people above all. They responded to both people and issues in a consistently caring, responsible way. They were not self-centered or unreliable. Their approaches to life were characterized by a consistent effort to be kind and fair.

In short, they had both reached a high level of psychological maturity, which their similar choices and priorities reflected. Their personalities and philosophies were inseparable, all of a piece. Now all Ron and Ingrid needed to complete their personal goals was a suitable mate.

As Ron drove Ingrid back home and parted with her more affectionately than before, they were both beginning to think the search had ended. Ron and Ingrid had started their third date by building bookcases and finished it by falling in love.

# Chapter Eight

## CLOSE ENCOUNTERS
## OF THE FOURTH KIND

### *Making Your Move and Getting Sexual*

You have developed a warm, enjoyable relationship with potential for romance in which you can share ideas, philosophies, interests and concerns. You are now ready to consider sexually intimate contact and to determine whether your newly developed friendship can move in this direction. In making decisions about sexual invitations which you hope could lead eventually to a life commitment, you need to think about several issues:

- how to intitate a sexual relationship so that it maximizes the potential for further screening and movement toward your goal of commitment.
- how to communicate an informal arrangement with your new love interest so that, if he or she is not right for you, you can maintain a friendship or at least good feelings if you should find that you are not compatible as mates.
- how to weed out an unloving, emotionally dishonest candidate with no debts or regrets, despite any former understanding made in good faith.

71

- how to determine whether you and your love interest are emotionally and sexually compatible after you are confident that you are dealing with a basically honest, loving person.

## Initiating a Sexual Relationship

In dealing with sexual attraction, it is best to remember that you are not in a movie role, stranded together on some desert island, or swept off your feet at a Cinderella ball or other such episodes of high adventure and romance whereupon, at the cue of the director, you both instantly recognize your urgent desire for one another. In real life you have to consider your values and feelings and those of your prospective partner.

You don't want to feel hurt or rejected; nor would you be fair in passing those feelings on to another. This is a touchy issue in more ways than one. Therefore, before you touch, you should consider the fact that non-verbal cues and responses will not help you very much in understanding your partner's attitudes and feelings nor in communicating your own.

Your best insurance against causing an embarrassing scene is to talk before moving further on to intimacy. Sexual feelings are laden with complex social values and background experiences which can only be communicated, at least initially, through language.

Talk about your thoughts and feelings and get your partner's reactions. If your partner makes the first sexual advance before you've had a chance to exchange values and motives in this area, it is perfectly appropriate to slow down the action until you both can agree upon its direction and pace. Though many formulas for sexual behavior and timing in relationships have been popularized since the "modern" 1920's (heavily influenced by Henry Ford's invention of a bedroom on wheels), there is no "right" formula for *when* you should become sexually intimate.

The mid-sixties put an end to the notion of "experienced" men and virginal women and all the sexual protocols necessary (kissing, "necking", and "petting") before "going all the way." However, while many have hailed the simplification of an "all or nothing" approach, and the acceptance of premarital sex as an integral part of a mature relationship, considerable pressure is placed on couples to engage in sexual intercourse before they talk regarding this sensitive issue. Without mutual understanding, couples are left wide open to disappointments and even exploitation by sexual partners.

One age-old method of getting around these dangers which is still used by people with strict, fundamentalist values is to postpone sex until marriage. However, people who choose this approach have to consider the fact that they have far less opportunity to explore mutual compatibility in the most important area of a heterosexual relationship—sexual love. Those who abstain until marriage are also taking a far greater emotional risk if problems surface in marriage which were previously masked as virtues in the area of self-restraint.

For that reason among others, most people today are willing to take the necessary emotional risks in seriously attempting to develop a fulfilling sexual relationship with another which could lead to a lifetime experience. However, if you have any common sense or self-esteem, you obviously want to avoid people who cannot give mature love to you or anyone because of personality problems which they either cannot see or refuse to acknowledge. You have the right and the personal obligation to end these relationships immediately and continue your search for a person with the capacity to love.

## See No Evil

Like the proverbial Chinese monkey who saw no evil, one of the dangers of sexual attraction is that it can make you vulnerable to a good sales pitch which offers little substance and masks some serious problems. Prospective home buyers, for example, learn to be wary of the "handyman's special." Billed as a "great buy that just needs minor repairs" by a manipulative real estate agent, the house, in actuality, is generally no more than a crumbling shell. The cost of repairs far exceeds the amount which could be recouped by resale of the property at a later date.

Similarly, in considering a prospective mate, one popular myth which you should yank out by its roots is the notion that "all you need is love." If some of the best talent in the field, such as the Old Testament

Prophets, Jesus Christ, and Gautama Buddha knew better than to attempt to reform certain desperate cases, you might want to examine your own level of saintliness if you should feel tempted to undertake this feat.

Furthermore, if you are gifted in the area of helping others there are numerous social services agencies, churches, and other community organizations which go begging for competent personnel. However, if you enter one of these fields and become a psychologist, social worker, counselor, minister or other such professional, the first thing you will learn is that, for ethical reasons and for the sake of your own mental health, you should *never* become sexually involved with your clients. Dilapidated houses are problems for experts in the building profession, and broken personalities are best helped by experts in the mental health professions.

## Selective Sexuality

Sexual relationships are generally the "acid test" in sizing up a person's total personality. Sometimes an individual we initially like and feel sexually attracted to in the early stages of dating slips through our filtering screen and turns out to be a disaster in bed. Let's look at some personality types which should start the signs over your emergency exit door flashing.

## Kinks and Kooks

These individuals usually—but not always—show themselves up before the sexual stage of a relationship, if you are alert to their attitudes and behavior in the earlier stages. Unfortunately, in some cases, the only way you can see the dark side of a kink's or kook's otherwise normal image is through sexual involvement. While these people deserve compassion for whatever tragic experience produced their problems, they are not automatically entitled to the time, energy, and hopes of an innocent bystander with normal needs and expectations who had nothing to do with creating their painful situation.

74

The responsibility for getting treatment, or a willing partner with similar problems, belongs to *them*, not you. In fairness to you, they owe you all the facts *before* you get into bed. If you ever encounter one of these types in a sexual situation, you have a right to feel violated and an obligation to terminate the relationship immediately.

## *Setting Kinks Straight*

Most people would know what to do if they entered someone's bedroom for the first time and found it cluttered with whips, handcuffs, and black leather boots—remove themselves immediately, and screen all further calls on their answering machine to be sure that personal contact with that individual is severed.

Such extreme situations are highly unlikely. Individuals with very unusual sexual tastes tend to stay in close-knit groups with others of similar inclinations. However, it could happen that during very early stages of your sexual relationship you become uncomfortable because your partner insists upon one or both of you wearing certain garments or acting out fantasies which entail unusual behavior.

You are definitely no prude by refusing to engage in such behavior and you certainly need to call an immediate halt to the relationship. While there is no problem with individuals in a secure, loving, long-term relationship mutually agreeing to some form of harmless sexual novelty, people who need to *begin* a relationship with this sort of thing are not relating to you at all. You deserve to be appreciated and made love to for your own sake, not because you evoke a partner's erotic fantasies with whatever prop turns him or her on.

Jenny, for example, was amused at first when Carl teased her into wearing the crotchless pair of nylons be bought her as a "gag gift." The situation lost its humor, however, when he consistently insisted upon her wearing them on subsequent occasions to the point of sulking, implying prudishness on her part, and rejecting her sexually when she refused.

She wisely refrained from creating any further unpleasantness by writing Carl a sympathetic but firm note explaining she was ending the relationship because he had owed her an explanation of his sexual inclinations *before* he had become sexually involved with her. She gave

75

him the benefit of the doubt by suggesting that perhaps he had been afraid or ashamed to admit his reliance upon provocative garments to become aroused. However, she made it clear that this possibility did not absolve his responsibility to be honest with her so that she could have left herself open for a more pleasant and aring experience with another man. She suggested that in the future Carl either obtain therapy or confine himself to sexual partners who *verbally* express inclinations similar to his by discussing his fetishes before, not after, engaging in sex with them.

Jenny ended her note by making it clear that she wanted no further contact with Carl. She recognized the fact that Carl's problems with sex made it impossible for him to be truly attracted to her or to relate to her feelings and needs. More importantly, she knew she could not play "sex therapist" even if Carl had wanted to change (and she had seen no indication in his behavior that he did). Although she was a little angry and upset after the experience she realized that she had learned some valuable information about sexual hang-ups and resolved to be more careful in these areas *before* becoming sexually involved with the next man who seemed to have potential as a prospective mate.

## *Curtailing Kooky Behavior*

Many people feel ambivalent about sex and attempt to deal with their negative feelings by enacting certain rigid rituals. Frank found himself involved with such a type when he became sexual with Ann. He had regarded her as a lovely, vivacious woman who seemed to look forward to their romance. However, though she was passionate during love-making, her mood changed immediately after his orgasm and she seemed to be counting the minutes until she could extract herself from his embrace and rush to the bathroom to cleanse herself. In attempting to talk to Ann about her behavior, Frank found that she became evasive or turned the gist of the conversation into an issue of *his* problems with her behavior.

On their next date, Frank took Ann on a long walk in the park in order to have a talk about her problem with accepting men—a problem he felt neither competent nor willing to put up with. Ann said she did not want to end the relationship and attempted to assure him that in time the problem would "go away." Yet over the course of their conversation it became clear that Ann had been waiting for her problem to "go away" for 15 years. Ann's "treatment plan" not only left something to be desired in terms of overcoming her compulsive behavior, but she also demonstrated a total lack of sensitivity for or awareness of the feelings and needs of the other person in a relationship.

Frank explained that he simply could not and would not begin a relationship in which he was not fully accepted as a man. He suggested that Ann seek counseling before attempting further relationships, while assuring her that she had a great deal to offer a man when she could clear up her conflicts. Despite their disappointment, they parted with a friendly understanding.

## Reality Therapy

Both Jenny and Frank realized that reality was the best and most compassionate attitude they could convey to their respective partners; in these two cases, the reality of their own feelings and needs which Carl and Ann could in no way fulfill. Luckily for Jenny and Frank, individuals whose sexual problems involve fetishes or compulsive behavior are easy to detect.

However, let's consider several more insidious types who can waste much more of your time and inflict considerably more pain if you don't call their hand. Reality works best upon them as well. However, they are skilled at manipulating the cards: it's more difficult to see they're not playing with a full deck.

## Six Types Worth Avoiding

There are several features common to all of these types. Though they have different styles, they specialize in degrading their partner in sexual love. They are masters of manipulation who prefer to work exclusively with considerate, decent people, because their "own kind" would be on to them so fast they wouldn't have time to experience the only real climax they understand—the sting.

77

Like the more obvious problem-types described earlier, these people have hang-ups rooted in unfortunate background experiences. The most critical common factor is that they fear or dislike people of the opposite sex due to some real or imagined injury sustained in childhood. In matters of love their primary drive is revenge. In their minds, no matter how guilty they really are or claim to be over their behavior, they believe that you deserve what you get for being stupid enough to believe in love.

For this reason, it is difficult for partners to be compassionate with those who have character disorders, except in the abstract, because when these types are effective, their injuries leave barely enough resources for fight or flight. The most important thing to know about these individuals is not whether they can't or won't help what they do, but that they didn't help what they did before they did it to *you*.

Before examining the individual styles of this group it is important to point out that they are the masters of oap opera scenarios. As fire is the best way to fight fire, your best method of exposing writers of "soap scenes" is to clean up the act with extra-strength reality—who you are and why a nice person like you does not belong with a person like this.

## *Recognizing a "Set-Up"*

CONS operate on the principle of betrayal. Their m.o. consists of luring you into emotional dependency through short-term fulfillment. They appear sensitive, passionate, and solicitous of your every need. They seem to anticipate your every want. Cons pay special attention to your hopes. They seduce you with insubstantial samples of everything you *could* have in a relationship with them, *if* you can forgive them for cheating on you, or *if* you can believe that their overnight with so-and-so was really spent in a platonic discussion about nuclear disarmament.

The bottom line with cons is that if you want a relationship with them, you must be willing to accept whatever outrageously disloyal activity they can concoct in their ever-scheming brains. They are the proverbial naughty children caught with their hands in the cookie jar; they rely upon the "*con*version principle" to maintain relationships. You must learn to believe that their hearts are on the path to truth and light but that their hands just lingered somewhere behind. "To err is human but to forgive divine," must be the motto of a con's martyred partner.

Your best defense against the "evangelism" of cons is to realize that loving relationships are built upon a *record* of integrity, not deceit, disloyalty and ever-increasing demands for you to advance further trust when they prove untrustworthy. Cons promise love but give shame. As an old proverb states: "Fool me once, shame on you. Fool me twice, shame on me."

## *Corralling Coys*

COYS are the proverbial Tess and Tex the Teases. Like cons, they are basically arrested children in the often well-endowed bodies of adults. They are extraordinarily seductive, building you up to a fever pitch and torturing you with "come-ons" before beating a hasty retreat, leaving you with the alluring promise of "next time." Fortunately, in today's sexual climate, coys don't fare as well as they did when stricter moral standards against premarital sex were a feeding ground for their immature capers.

After you have suffered through several intimate candle-lit dinners and breathy hearth-side discussions on a sumptuous sofa only to find that by the end of the evening nothing ever happened, you can safely conclude that you are dealing with Tess or Tex in one of their many manifestations. The best method for rounding them up and moving them out is to understand that anyone who plays with your desires in a relationship has an agenda that is less than loving.

Brand them with indelicate honesty about your lack of interest in what is "over yonder." You owe it to yourself to leave Tess or Tex tethered to their own infantile behavior while you roam the range for more suitable prospects. Stick to your decision even though it is highly likely that your tease will appear contrite and ready to "give in." Like cons, coys' games end when no one will be their stooge in a new round. Their desperation to keep you is motivated not by love, but by the sexual power they hope to hold over you.

## Ending Rat Races

Behaviorism, a school of psychology based upon "shaping" behavior through controlled rewards, is fairly new. However, the practice of training people in much the same manner as circus poodles has been around a long time. Sexual love is highly vulnerable to this type of manipulation. We can speculate that the first people to discover the effectiveness of using sex to obtain what they wanted were cave-dwelling CONDITIONERS, who sported the best mastodon coats or saber-tooth jewelry as testaments of their accomplishments.

As crass as they are, modern conditioners have been bolstered by some very mixed-up values which have actually encouraged people to turn sexual love into the equivalent of a rat maze or trained poodle act.

Stereotypes have flourished about the proverbial female "headache" which miraculously disappears when some very expensive gift is produced or difficult favor rendered. However, men are just as likely to employ these degrading manipulations in a relationship.

Conditioners operate at a much pettier level than the disloyal con or the maddening tease. They seek to maintain a level of frustration just under their partners' limits of tolerance, but in the long run their price can be higher because naive partners can invest heavily in the relationship before wising up.

Marriage or live-in arrangements are a conditioner's cup of tea because these situations provide a more controlled environment for their training program. They often use initial sexual rewards to move the relationship in these directions. Conditioners can't spontaneously enjoy love because they need to control its outcome. They rarely have remorse for their hidden agendas. They feel you owe them something for their "giving up" their time and energy to you in sex.

They dole out sexual favors like dog yummies when they decide that you are "being good." In contrast to cons and coys, who behave like children, conditioners behave like parents—bad parents. Whether the idea is based on fact or fiction, they imagine that as youngsters they were treated similarly to the way they are treating you in the present. They want to be in the driver's seat in all future relationships to avoid any chance of that happening again.

If you are beginning to feel used in your new relationship, keep a close inventory of the circumstances surrounding your lovemaking episodes. Does your partner enjoy you spontaneously for your own sake or do things only warm up after you've done something he or she wanted? Jerry, for example, made a connection that Nora's warm and cold days could be directly related to the number of yard chores he volunteered to do for her. Sandy noted a similar correlation in Rick's amorous advances on days when she cut the last quarter of her evening class in order to make him a special dinner.

The key to a conditioner's behavior is that it is *always* self-serving and detrimental to the basic integrity and growth potential of the other person. Ask yourself if being a trained poodle is what you had in mind when you undertook the quest for a lifetime relationship.

If the answer is no, then use that excellent word on your conditioning partner when he or she suggests meeting again. (If you want to be polite you can say, "No, thank you.") Ignore manipulations to maintain an emotional hold on you and look for partners who want to share a relationship with a human being, not a household pet.

## Returning Clods to the Earth from Whence They Came

CLODS are easily identified by their insufferable behavior. They specialize in "put-down" remarks and boorish scenes designed to humiliate their partners both in intimate situations and in public. Due to the popularity of sexist humor, such as the "Take my wife" or the "woman driver" jokes, men are more frequently associated with this behavior. However, clods are actually well-represented by both sexes, and all social classes. The most genteel, pedigreed members of a community can be complete oafs in the area of sexual love. Demeaning, insulting, and depreciating attitudes toward a sexual partner, regardless of the wit or sophistication of delivery, bear the unmistakable mark of the clod.

Clods are famous for deliberately insensitive behavior in intimate situations. The classic Roll-over Rollo, or his counterpart Tidy Tina, changing the sheets and hoisting her pleasure machine out for the day, couldn't care less about their partner's feelings after getting what they wanted. Clods are also known for pairing erotic behavior with belittling remarks such as calling attention to the pimple they've discovered during foreplay.

Clods love to circulate their so-called love interest in social gatherings so that their polished ridicule can be appreciated by an audience. They can be counted upon to disclose embarrassing information about their partners, especially after he or she has received a compliment at the party.

When Bert was slapped on the shoulder by his business associate, and told that he looked especially fit, his date Nadine couldn't miss the chance to exclaim hilariously: "Oh, that's just because he's wearing his so-called back brace. You know, a man's version of a corset."

When fair-haired Cathy was informed by an admiring acquaintance she looked "positively radiant," her partner Tony piped in, "She ought to. She uses enough bleach to light up Chicago."

If you want to feel as if you are too tall or short, too fat or thin, or that you are not quite as good as a former lover in bed (name, description of physical endowments and sexual prowess supplied by your cloddish partner), then hold on to your clod at any cost. He or she will never let you forget how lucky you are to have found someone charitable enough to be seen with the likes of you.

However, if you believe that you possess qualities worthy of respect and appreciation, then the thought of dropping the clod and dusting off your hands is also worthy of your consideration—and *immediate* follow-through. Where clods are concerned, resist your first healthy impulse, which is to kill them, and act on your second, more practical impulse, which is to dump them.

## *Letting Ships of the Desert Sail Without You*

CAMELS are particularly emotionally sadistic in sexual relationships because, unlike most red-blooded people, they have mastered the art of "going for a long time between drinks." They are able to perform quite adequately as sexual partners *when* they want to. However, their primary motive in finding a mate is to entrap a sexually normal person within the heterosexual bond in order to withhold sex.

Reducing a mature person with normal needs to a state of quiet or vocalized hysteria is the thing that really turns a camel on. Only then can he or she feel supreme and inviolate while the partner, in the mind of the camel, is cast in the role of a frenzied four-legged creature during a heat cycle.

Camels are difficult to detect initially because generally they will reserve their full-blown withholding behavior until after commitments have been exchanged and considerable energy (yours) invested. In the beginning of a relationship they can be quite amorous, but once they feel secure they've got you, they begin their passive-aggressive torture techniques.

Before wasting enough time and devotion on a camel to enable him or her to feel secure enought to go on a sexual strike, you should be alert to behavior which, when pieced together, begins to form a specific profile. The following traits should help you discern whether you have indeed found the Arabian prince or princess of your dreams, or merely one of their steeds.

- Camels generally don't have close, supportive relationships even with members of their own sex.
- They are awkward about expressing spontaneous emotion and they either choose a superior or inferior role in their social interactions.
- Camels tend to equate adulthood with rigid, stuffy, sanctimonious behavior. When they do express emotion, they appear immature, slightly silly, and inappropriate.
- Camels like to justify opportunistic behavior which puts them at an advantage over others. They veer away from intimacy, warmth, sharing, generosity, and social equality.
- Camels like things which will enhance their self-image. A partner may be temporarily part of that process—at least until he or she acts too much like a person and ceases to function as a piece of furniture in the camel's interior decor.

- When camels can't reduce threats to their egotistical self-images, they will build themselves up at their partner's expense by reducing someone they supposedly love to his or her lowest levels through the frustration of one of the most basic adult needs in a heterosexual relationship—sexual love.

Insecure, insensitive, self-centered people can leave you stuck for a long time between water holes, with the dubious comfort of one mirage after another which turns to sand as soon as you get close. To hop off this caravan, you have only to say the magic words: *Mature Love.* Isn't that what you wanted when you started on this journey? It's still yours for the taking if you steer clear of camels.

## *Can'ts*

This group is the most heart-rending of all and deserves some gentleness and respect. In fairness to you, a "Can't" should not agree to a relationship which is mutually regarded as having serious potential. However, Can'ts may delude themselves into believing that a serious relationship with the right person may be all they need to solve their problems.

Can'ts range from true virgins who have just been too frightened of sex to get to this stage in a relationship, to people with long-term sexual difficulties, to sexually normal people who have recently undergone a serious trauma and have not recovered. Can'ts aren't usually out to hurt anyone, or arrogant enough to want to impose their hang-ups on another. They just want to be loved, and believe love might cure them of their problem.

The catch is that it won't. As has been stated before, love and psychotherapy do *not* mix—and the latter is what Can'ts really need. Beginning a love relationship with marriage potential requires *two* people in good sexual/emotional shape. It cannot be a haven or refuge for people to collect themselves so they can practice taking the most basic risks of adult life. Serious heterosexual relationships require a *record* of strength in the area of sexual love.

If you take the time to develop a trusting friendship in which sexual values and background histories can be discussed *before* entering into the sexual stage, you will probably draw out the virginal type of Can't with little trouble, and you may be lucky enough to spot the other two as well. This situation is a vast improvement over an awkward, unfulfilling sexual encounter or, even worse, several of them. It is better both for you and for the Can'ts because they don't have to experience another sexual failure and subsequent rejection. Moreover, you don't have to wonder if something about you turned them off, or to extract some painful confession from them in an effort to find out what is going wrong.

Can'ts, unless they are extremely dishonest with themselves and others, will generally provide clues in their conversations about their pasts, which, if probed gently, can tell you all you need to know before you try an encounter of the fourth kind. However, sometimes you may miss something important and find yourself in an awkward situation with a Can't.

## Mitch Strikes Out with Vicky

Vicky found herself in such a predicament with Mitch. She felt shaken and confused after an hour of unsuccessful lovemaking— unsuccessful on Mitch's part at least because she had felt completely carried away before it became obvious he was not. She knew she had been patient and unpressuring. After all, first times with someone were always a little awkward. She also liked to believe that she could compete with any geisha when it came to techniques for turning a man on.

She was totally bewildered. What was wrong with her? She was jolted out of her preoccupation with her own feelings by Mitch's deep sigh, which almost sounded like a sob. She suddenly realized he was extremely depressed. Concerned, she murmured a few supportive assurances while maneuvering a change of scene from the bedroom, where tragedy seemed to hover around Mitch like an impenetrable cloud, to her well-lighted, cheerful kitchen. As she made idle conversation and a pot of tea, she watched him protectively as he slowly came back to the present moment.

When he was settled comfortably, sipping tea, and responding with some of his usual vibrancy, she took a deep breath and got ready to say, "Mitch, let's talk about this." But before she could speak, he said, "I know. We need to talk about what happened."

In the conversation that followed, Vicky realized she had missed a clue on their third date by not following through on her first impulse to probe the circumstances of Mitch's divorce and the brief amount of transition time he had allowed himself before beginning a serious relationship with her.

Now he was opening all this up to her in a flood of painful information. Mitch had never experienced problems with sex in his ten-year marriage. However, he had been seriously traumatized by learning of his wife's many extra-marital affairs during one of their fights leading to the marital break-up. He found himself, for the first time, beginning to doubt himself as a man. Sensing her advantage, his former wife had played upon his fears and further taunted him in this area.

The final straw, however, occurred when he sought to prove himself immediately after their separation by becoming involved with the first woman who looked twice at him. After several of these casual relationships in fairly rapid succession, he found that his confidence was failing. And, for the first time, he was experiencing impotence. He decided he simply was not going after the right kind of relationships. He had desperately wanted his marriage to work, and hoped to replace his terrible loss with a good marriage in order, as he put it, "to wipe out the past as soon as possible." He had felt so lucky to have met Vicky, who had qualities he had always dreamed of. He realized that he should have paid more attention to what his body was telling him in his most recent relationships before meeting her, but in a burst of confidence, which Vicky had inspired, he just hadn't believed there could be any problem when he was with her.

Vicky and Mitch talked for a long time, arriving at the conclusion that Mitch was rushing himself way too fast. By not giving himself transition time to grieve for the loss of his ideal wife (the one who had existed only in his mind), and to heal his emotional injuries, he was only creating worse problems for himself. He had started relationships off on the wrong foot by trying to replace his first bad relationship with a second.

When he was content to involve himself with casual relationships in which no emotional investments were expected from the woman, at least he was hurting only himself. However, by believing he could cover his wounds with a new love, he had nearly passed his loss of confidence on to Vicky.

As they both knew, this was the last thing Vicky needed. It had not been so long ago that *she* had felt like raw meat herself, due to a painful divorce. However, unlike Mitch, she had resisted the immediate impulse to go frantically looking for a replacement marriage, and had given herself time to heal and recoup her self-esteem.

Mitch and Vicky realized they had many characteristics in common which looked promising for a good relationship, but their timing was off. Mitch was a good year away from being ready; he needed to work through the wreckage of a ten-year marriage. Mitch realized it was time he treated himself to a good psychotherapist. He had been trying to pull himself up by his own bootstraps long enough.

It took his fear of hurting Vicky to make Mitch realize just how hurt he still was himself. Both Mitch and Vicky parted as better people from the experience, and promised to keep in touch from time to time. Six months later, they talked again by telephone and exchanged news and views.

Vicky was seeing a "wonderful man," as she described him, and they were planning their engagement party. Mitch had found an excellent therapist who was not only helping him to heal the divorce experience, but also, as he put it, "helping me clear out a lot of other deadwood."

He no longer had any sexual problems, which, as both Mitch and Vicky suspected, were only the tip of the iceberg, but he still didn't feel ready to begin a serious relationship. "The truth is," he said, "I'm still too scared of being hurt again. But hearing about your good luck gives me so much hope. We had a lot of things in common and that makes me think that if you can do it, someday soon so can I."

87

## Taking the Worry Out of Being Close

Through these two simple techniques—selectivity and reality focus—you can save yourself an enormous amount of misspent time, energy and emotions. At about two years of age when it suddenly occurred to you that you were a separate entity from all others and capable of exerting control, you learned one of the most important words of your life: *No.* Now, with the wisdom of an adult, true to your own feelings and goals, you can use this word with great effectiveness to screen out anyone arrogant enough to think he or she can run your life, or confused enough to velieve tat he or she is ready for a serious relationship when that isn't the case.

As a final word of caution, however, let us slip into the role of your high school gym teacher and remind you that in regard to your physical well-being, modern medicine has not been successful in taking the worry out of being close. For your physical as well as your mental health, it is critical for you to determine the level of honesty and responsibility of a potential sexual partner. Sadly, an epidemically large number of people have fallen short in this area.

It is possible in your dating experience that you either have or will come across someone with a sexually communicable disease. By learning to select dating partners of good character, you should, of course, first find this out *before* any sexual contact is initiated.

## Education and Information

Two major precautions should be exercised if you want to be responsible to yourself and others in sexual relationships:

(1) If you haven't already done so, you should obtain medical information, preferably from a clinic specializing in human sexuality and public health, about prevention of pregnancy and sexually communicable diseases.

(2) Before having intimate relations, you should give yourself time to know your partner and feel comfortable about discussing your respective pasts, which inevitably will include, at least in broad terms, your sexual histories.

88

Disease prevention is obviously not the sole reason why you need this information. If you are protective enough about your emotional welfare and about the rights of others, you will be in good hands when you make decisions which could affect your physical well-being. It is crucial from many vantage points to know whether your partner has had a history of multiple relationships, or whether he or she has chosen to be selective before meeting you.

Many serious mate seekers, perhaps including yourself, have gone through phases of multiple relationships, or serial relationships. You need to determine from the information you obtain from a potential partner's past, whether her or she is ready to become monogamous for the right reasons. You also need to know whether a potential partner has a clean bill of health. If a prospective partner has had a recent history of multiple sexual relationships, or other health risks, you need to discuss this and try to determine, perhaps in consultation with a doctor, whether there is a risk that he or she is carrying a transmissible disease.

In obtaining past information you may encounter people who have tried life-styles which could be hazardous from many perspectives. For many reasons besides sexual safety, you want to be very wary of a potential partner who has been an intravenous drug user. A male bi-sexual is also a risk emotionally and physically.

You may find a serious mate seeker who informs you at the outset that he or she has a viral disease, such as herpes, which may be only mildly disabling to the infected individual and controllable in terms of infecting others. Because this virus is incurable, many very fine but less fortunate people than yourself are forced to carry on a normal life with this extra burden.

If you meet someone with a chronic disease of this type, who appears otherwise promising, you should obtain as much medical information as possible from your doctor, your partner's doctor, or a clinic specializing in this area before considering any moves toward intimacy. Because you are considering this person for a mate, not a date, you should make sure that your questions include health issues which could affect your entire life—your own health, reproduction (if you should want children), and so on.

Individuals who have been infected in the past with any diseases which could be infectious with intimate contact, also need to furnish medical information which makes it possible for you, in consultation with a doctor, to determine the level of safety to yourself or offspring if you should ultimately marry.

As we all know from media coverage, in the case of the AIDS virus, individuals in the process of the syndrome face catastrophic, terminal illness. At the present time there is still much to be learned about the effects on those exposed to the virus who have not developed the Acquired Immune Deficiency Syndrome. Heterosexuals, especially those who are selective about their partners, who are not involved with group intravenous drug use or sexual partners such as prostitutes who may be involved with the drug culture, are presently in a low-risk group for contracting the AIDS virus. However, don't take our word in this ever-changing area of research. You need to rely upon the most current public health information to be adequately informed. To determine your level of risk and the best ways to minimize these risks, you need continually to update your knowledge of this issue by consulting medically qualified publications. Reports based upon studies conducted by experts in disease prevention and control are the best sources of public health information. These reports interpret data from large, representative population samples. Speculative opinion with no empirical foundation, or interpretations of data from small, select samples which do not represent the general population, are not reliable sources of information regardless of media attention. Be wary of opinions which are not supported by medical evidence.

You need to know and to anticipate all physical and mental health risks which could be involved in an intimate relationship without getting sidetracked by attitudes based upon hysteria rather than reason. A *thoroughly informed* period of consideration enables you, if you so choose, to enter into a sexual relationship with security, pleasure, and hope.

It is also worth pointing out that those who may be using the spectre of sexually communicable diseases, such as AIDS, to justify staying in a destructive relationship or latching onto anyone just to get married and "out of circulation", might feel less secure if they reviewed the history of syphilis. The spread of that once devastating and once terminal disease, prior to the advent of antibiotics, was not prevented by marriage or strict Victorian moral standards. People who did not choose to be honest and responsible with their mates carried right on with their multiple relationships, passing on the infection with abandon to their families.

Your best health insurance, physically and mentally, is in learning to find a mature, loving, healthy individual who sincerely wants to share a monogamous lifetime relationship with you.

## A Fourth Worth Celebrating

Now, armed with all of these "what to do if" possibilities, let's move on to a more promising scenario and take a "fly on the picnic basket" peek at Ron and Ingrid, who we left falling in love at the end of a "philosophy date."

Two months later, we see them sitting cozily together in a park for an afternoon picnic in honor of "Interdependence Day," as they have chosen to call their personal celebration. Between apple wedges and sips of champagne they find themselves reminiscing about the flat tire, the stencilled bookshelf (now overflowing with Dr. Seuss books which gaily decorate Donna's weekend bedroom), and their easy transition from sharing their values, hopes, and dreams to sharing themselves.

These two seasoned veterans of rejection in their former relationships had learned their lessons well. In the school of unfulfilling relationships, their self-centered, sexually immature partners had taught them that the only good thing about suffering is that it could convince one to learn how *not* to suffer.

Because their mistakes had been etched in their minds by unhappy experiences in love, they promised themselves nothing but a caring, empathic relationship with a competent person in the future. Moreover, they each took the first step in placing themselves in their *own* competent hands until they could find someone with equal maturity and sincerity.

Thanks to their diligent completion of "know thyself" homework assignments after every date up to the time they met each other, each

91

was able to spot the key themes to a successful relationship—responsibility and integrity—in the other. Because they were able to respond to each other's values and aspirations in an intimate relationship, they were able to move easily into sharing their sexual feelings and the meaning they placed upon this kind of intimacy.

Their own self-confidence as well as their mature, empathic approach to each other enabled them to take the calculated risks necessary in fostering sexual love. They were able to lay their minds and then their hearts and bodies on the line, despite fears and doubts based on former mistakes, because they trusted their own good judgment.

Now, as they click their plastic cups and watch the shadows grow long with the sinking sun, they know they're celebrating the fruits of their personal efforts. They know there are no guarantees for continuing their fulfilling relationship except their mutual willingness to maintain their own good character and foster their love. However, they each suspect that they are on to something great—and so do we.

# Chapter Nine

## HITTING A SNAG: HOW TO AVOID SETTLING FOR SOMEONE YOU DON'T REALLY WANT

### *Am I—or Am I Not—In Love?*

Suppose you've been seeing someone seriously for a number of months and you can't understand why you still hesitate to make a commitment. You begin asking yourself whether you're really in love. If you feel reluctant to commit, your mind is sending you an important signal to which you should pay strict attention. There are three possible answers.

### *1. Dumb Hang-Ups—Jeff Wonders if Deirdre Is Pretty Enough*

Jeff had a problem about Deirdre. She seemed to be the woman of his dreams. Deirdre shared Jeff's passion for the opera, she too wanted to have children, she had a delightful personality, and their sexual experiences together were thrilling. Jeff felt that he loved Deirdre and thought he should consider himself the luckiest man alive. He wondered, then, why he had twice postponed asking her out to choose an engagement ring. Jeff decided to confide his bewilderment to his sensible older brother Gordon, who was also his best friend.

93

"It's just that I keep thinking Deirdre isn't attractive enough," he
began.

Gordon raised an eyebrow. He had met Deirdre and considered her
exceptionally pretty. Why weren't her good looks adequate from Jeff's
point of view? Gordon asked Jeff jokingly whether he felt he needed a
movie star for a wife.

Jeff already understood that his one lingering reservation about
Deirdre was ridiculous. He and Gordon discussed a number of possible
explanations. Jeff was a level-headed fellow of 28. It didn't seem likely
that he was still entertaining juvenile fantasies of marrying the
breathtaking poster girls whose photos adorned his bedroom when he
was a teenager. Gordon suggested that perhaps Jeff associated beauty
with status and wanted to impress people by means of a ravishing mate.
Jeff sat up straight in his chair: this explanation rang a bell.

In fact, Jeff had recently suffered some minor business setbacks and
he had temporarily been feeling insecure about his abilities. Perhaps he
wanted a glamorous wife to compensate for his self-doubt or to dazzle
clients he was (unnecessarily) afraid of losing. Gordon reminded him
that his business difficulties were slight and already diminishing. He
had no reason for long-term worry. He also recalled Jeff's outstanding
record in business school and his speedy promotions since taking his
present job. Jeff brightened. There was, after all, no valid foundation
for his self-doubt; he felt it begin to evaporate.

Jeff's illuminating talk with his brother put his reservation about
Deirdre in perspective. He realized that the problem had actually been
within himself all along. Once he and Gordon identified it, his
reluctance ceased to exist.

As Jeff returned home, relieved, he felt the need to talk to his other
best friend, his future wife Deirdre. Now he wanted to set a date,
without further delay, for their ring-buying expedition.

## Rhonda Worries that Eric May Be Too Much Like Her Father

Rhonda, age 24, developed a similarly unfounded hesitation about naming a date for the wedding her fiance Eric wanted as soon as possible. While waiting at the hairdresser's one evening when she was tired and impressionable, Rhonda had skimmed an article in a magazine which advised women to avoid marrying men who too closely resembled their fathers. Rhonda became worried; she had had a painful relationship with her harsh, domineering father. She pondered whether Eric reminded her of him in any way. Then she thought with alarm of his freckles. Eric, like Rhonda's father, had a spray of freckles across his nose. Rhonda considered this similarity and found herself becoming more nervous after a few days passed. She decided to phone her friend Liz, a graduate student in psychology, to talk it over.

"Liz," she began breathlessly when she heard her friend answer, "I've developed a freckle phobia!" Rhonda went on to explain her worry about the connection between Eric and her father.

Liz laughed and asked Rhonda the crucial question: "Does Eric resemble your father in *personality*?"

It took Rhonda no time at all to frame her reply. "Of course not!" she declared. "Eric is gentle and considerate. My father had the sensitivity of Attila the Hun. Eric and he just couldn't be more different."

"Okay," said Liz, wrapping the matter up. "You've solved your own problem. Eric, like your father, has freckles and incidentally, so do millions of other people, including me. But he doesn't have your father's rotten character. That's what you were really worried about, isn't it?"

Rhonda had to giggle about the ludicrous nature of her suspicion. Freckles certainly didn't turn her sweet Eric into the tyrant of her childhood. She breathed a sigh of relief. "Liz," she asked, " how would you like to be my maid of honor for our wedding next month?"

Jeff and Rhonda both hesitated, briefly, because of groundless reservations which might better be called "dumb hang-ups." If you, too, seem to have lucked out with the genuine Mr. or Ms. Right and then suddenly find yourself obsessed over some insignificant detail that has nothing to do with the depth of your love or the soundness of your partner's character, it's time to get a little input from a reliable friend. You need to clarify your thinking, not to put the relationship "on hold."

These types of problems are "head" problems which can be solved with an application of proper perspective. Then you can confidently sound the "all clear" and proceed onward to marriage.

But what about obstacles to marriage that are *not* imaginary?

## 2. Reality Problems: Coping With the Unexpected

Any relationship, no matter how strong, will be tested when it encounters the unknown. Your happiness in finding the right mate does not guarantee that the two of you will be forever immune to problems of health, employment, or other life-crises that are often beyond anyone's ability to predict or prevent. These are genuine problems, "reality" problems such as all adults must face at various points in their lives. The good news is, of course, that now you have a helpmate with whom you can share the problem and who will assist you in resolving it.

### Frank and Beryl Tackle a Career Setback

During the blissful period of his engagement to Beryl, Frank's career hit an unexpected bump. A giant corporation bought up the company which employed him as an aeronautical engineer. Everyone in his division was abruptly laid off. At first Frank panicked. He suggested to Beryl over dinner that perhaps they should postpone their wedding indefinitely, as he no longer could assume the responsibilities of a breadwinner.

Beryl took a calmer approach. She reminded Frank that she still had a job, they both had a little money in the bank, and they owed no one; they would get by, no matter what. She also reminded Frank that his prospects for future employment were excellent—his job performance rating had always been outstanding, he had never lost a job before, and his area of specialization continued to be much in demand with other companies. She offered to help him update his professional resumé.

Frank began to cheer up. He had, after all, only lost a job—he hadn't lost a vital relationship. It was no catastrophe. Together, he and Beryl could lick this temporary setback in short order. Frank still worried, though, about their plans for starting a family as soon as possible.

"Let's go ahead with the wedding, as scheduled," Beryl suggested sensibly, "and we'll think about having children a little later, after you get another job."

Frank felt a surge of gratitude and appreciation for Beryl's warm, loving support and for her practical perspective. He thought for the thousandth time, but with renewed conviction, what an ideal wife he had found.

Frank ceased regarding himself as a blighted, jobless fellow. As he hugged Beryl, he said: "You know what? I'm really a very lucky man."

## Peter and Bernice Cope With a Health Problem

The problem Peter and Bernice found themselves facing just six weeks before their wedding day had both frightened at first. Bernice had recently been promoted on her job to a new level of decision-making responsibility. She enjoyed her new position, which she had worked hard to earn, but was feeling much more stress. Peter had noticed with alarm that she frequently couldn't sleep and seemed rather jumpy. He finally insisted she see the company doctor for a thorough check-up.

When Bernice walked into the restaurant where Peter was waiting for her after work, her face wore the look of doom. "What's the matter, honey?" he asked.

"It's my blood pressure," Bernice replied. "It's up sixty points from last year!"

Peter gulped, then breathed a sigh of relief. "That's not good, but I feared something worse," he explained. "High blood pressure is a manageable disease. Almost everyone on my mother's side of the family has it."

Bernice began to feel somewhat reassured. She had met everyone in Peter's family, from his mother to his aunts, uncles, and cousins. She knew that they all lived normal, even unusually active lives. Bernice and Peter began to discuss the medication the doctor had prescribed and programs

for stress reduction in which she could enroll. The health problem that had
seemed to Bernice to hang like a dark cloud over their upcoming marriage
began to assume the brighter aspect of a controllable phenomenon.

"The first step we're going to take," said Peter, taking charge of the
situation, "is to eliminate salt from your diet. I'm borrowing my
mother's no-salt cookbook and taking over the cooking until you feel
better. You can practice relaxation exercises while I cook."

Bernice smiled. "Sounds great to me," she accepted. "But what
about having children? I can't go through a pregnancy safely with my
blood pressure so high."

Peter agreed. Although they both wanted a child, it was clear they
would have to wait until Bernice's health improved. "Look at it this
way," said Peter cheerfully. "We'll have another year or so just to enjoy
each other before we become parents. Think of it as kind of an extended
honeymoon."

Bernice blew him a kiss across the table. "Let's skip dessert and walk
to the druggist's to get my prescription filled," she said. "I want to hold
your hand."

Bernice had learned, as did Frank in confiding his unemployment
anxieties, that two heads can think more calmly than one, especially
when two hearts are involved as well.

Unexpected "reality" problems such as the ones successfully
confronted by these two engaged couples represent a hurdle to be
negotiated, not a dead-end. Almost all crises of this nature can be
overcome by taking a few practical steps to address them and by being
patient. As their respective problems are resolved with the passage of
time, both Frank and Bernice can derive strength and comfort from the
loving, concerned presence of their partners. Both couples may have to
adjust to an uncomfortable situation for a while, but the reality of their
love is no problem. In fact, it has been confirmed.

There are actually only a few "reality" problems that can't be managed.

One such problem, fortunately rare in occurrence, is the genuine
catastrophe. What do you do if your beloved, say, develops terminal
cancer? You may still wish to marry—certainly you would want to
remain close—but whatever you do, you need to be fully aware that

there can be no real future for you together in this tragic instance. You must prepare yourself to grieve, to integrate this love experience as a cherished memory, and eventually to resumé your life.

Luckily, most "reality" problems that can't be managed are less drastic. This special category has more to do with *changed perceptions* than with life events. If you have failed to notice something unpromising about the man or woman in your life up to this point, it's time to notice now, quickly—and bail out.

### 3. *Late-Surfacing Problems of Defective Radar:* *Irene Says "No Dice" to Gil the Gambler*

Occasionally people make such a stunning impression in the initial phases of a relationship that they are able to sweep others off their feet for a surprising length of time. Irene thought for two months that she had found the man of her dreams in Gil. He shared her love of sports, he was always attentive, and he had an interesting job as a staff writer for a medical magazine.

However, as they drew near to considering engagement, Irene began to wonder seriously if she had missed some important negative clues in her early screening of Gil. Lately Gil was behaving strangely; he often arrived for their dates very late with only a lame excuse. Also, he received many phone calls at home which he would only answer in the study, carefully closing the door so Irene couldn't overhear. He had borrowed money from her twice, claiming old credit card debts. When his car was hauled away by an angry-looking man with a tow truck and Gil refused to answer questions about the incident, it was the last straw. Alarmed and suspicious, Irene unburdened herself at lunch to her motherly boss, Vivian.

"Well," said Vivian, "it's probably not another woman, since money alone seems to be involved. But he's certainly hiding something."

Irene nodded sadly, knowing she would have to end the relationship if she couldn't trust Gil. "Any idea what it might be?" she asked.

"He holds a responsible job," Vivian reflected, "so it's probably not drinking or drugs. Gil reminds me a lot of my ex-husband, Chuck.

99

Maybe it's another kind of addiction: gambling. Chuck could never leave a card game. He was always late, always broke, and always in debt up to his eyeballs to some rather nasty loan sharks."

Irene inhaled sharply. "That makes sense," she had to agree. "It explains Gil's furtive behavior perfectly, I'm afraid." She asked Vivian what had happened to Chuck.

"Like most compulsive gamblers, he got worse," Vivian replied drily. "I tried interesting him in Gamblers Anonymous, but Mr. Macho Man insisted his problem was under control. When he tried to mortgage our house after a spree at the casinos, I divorced him. As far as I know, he's still gambling. But not with *my* money."

Irene thanked Vivian for the help in coping with her changed perceptions about the stability of Gil's character. The prospect of having her life ruined by cards, lies, and debts did not appeal to Irene at all. She decided to cut her losses early instead of waiting as Vivian had done. She would begin by confronting Gil with his dishonesty and terminating the relationship at once.

When Irene dropped by his office after 5 p.m. to carry out her intention, the speech she had planned proved unnecessary—there was Gil in the back room, playing high-stakes poker with some sinister-looking characters. Irene walked out.

After a month or so of healing and taking stock, Irene resuméd her search for a lifetime partner, but this time with her mental radar tuned for maximum clarity. Meanwhile, she congratulated herself heartily for managing to avoid the certain disaster of marrying Gil the Gambler.

## Wanda the Workaholic Gets Fired

Harold encountered another type of late-surfacing problem as his relationship with Wanda entered its "getting serious" phase. They seemed to have a great deal in common, especially their passion for photography, and both had expressed the desire to have children within the near future. Harold knew Wanda was earnest about her career with a market research firm, just as he was about his position as an academic administrator. He admired her ambition. But he had no idea of its scope until Wanda breezed into his apartment one evening after a business trip.

"I've been promoted to assistant vice president!" she announced gaily.

Before Harold could congratulate her, Wanda added: "But it means I'll be based in Chicago."

Harold was flabbergasted. Chicago was far away and they had agreed early in their dating that, if marriage were considered, re-location would be ruled out. Harold liked his life and enjoyed his current job as dean of students at a small college. "You know I can't come with you to Chicago," he said soberly, resenting Wanda's acceptance of the promotion without even consulting him.

Wanda suggested a week-end relationship. "I could fly in to see you once or twice a month," she coaxed, adding, "unless I get really busy, of course."

Harold shook his head; he wanted a live-in mate, not an occasional visitor. Wanda had never before indicated she was so absorbed in her work. "And what about kids?" he asked.

"Well, I certainly can't take time out from my career for babies now that I'm on a roll, can I?" said Wanda cheerfully. "Don't you see? This promotion changes everything."

With regret, Harold agreed that it did. He began to explain to Wanda that the priorities she was now for the first time expressing were incompatible with his own. "I can't offer you what you want most, a high-powered career," he concluded gently. "And you can't offer me what I want most, a stable home with a family. We'd better redefine our relationship as friends."

Wanda reluctantly reached the same conclusion. "You're right. It's impossible," she admitted. "My career means more to me at present that any other consideration."

Harold and Wanda accepted each other's different priorities. They parted as friends, wished each other well, and promised to keep in touch.

As Harold thoughtfully sipped a bedtime cup of herbal tea, he reflected on the fond memories he still cherished of Wanda during the early days of their brief relationship. He was glad they hadn't been spoiled by a long-term commitment featuring violent clashes of priorities. Harold considered himself lucky that he had been able to prevent this clear case of irreconcilable differences, thanks to prompt identification of the problem as soon as Wanda announced her intention to relocate. Wanda perhaps could be happy with a fellow workaholic, but not with him. Harold felt proud that he had been true to himself, and to his own life-goals.

## Agnes Decides that Life with Merle the Miser Wouldn't Pay Off

Agnes, age 24, felt at first that she had found a really extraordinary fellow when she started dating Merle, a loan officer at the local bank. Unlike the more bohemian men she had met in art school, Merle was neat, financially solvent, and prompt. He didn't smoke or drink. He always wore a suit. He seemed the very model of Victorian respectability.

It was true that some of her friends had wisecracked that Merle sounded more like Mr. Clean than Mr. Right, but Agnes had paid no attention. Now, after two months of dating, she was beginning to wonder if Merle indeed had some rigid personality traits her friends had spotted and she perhaps had overlooked. She reviewed their dates to clarify her changing perceptions.

Whenever Merle asked Agnes out to eat, they seemed to wind up at the Methodist Church spaghetti dinner or the Elks Club pancake breakfast. At first she had simply thought he was remarkably civic-minded. Lately, though, Agnes had begun to suspect Merle was, well, not exactly the last of the big-time spenders. A dollar-fifty for "all you can eat" seemed to attract him like a moth to a flame.

Agnes finally detected a *pattern* in Merle's behavior she has failed to notice before. It all added up. He served day-old granola bread from the thrift bakery, tofu, and bean sprouts for lunch at his place not because he was a "health food enthusiast" but because it only cost pennies. (Merle even grew bean sprouts on the window sill.) The lighting in his living room couldn't really be called "intimate." It was downright dim, one lamp featuring a forty-watt bulb. His phone number was "unlisted" only because he didn't have a phone; Merle made his calls from the office. Finally, Merle even boasted of finding his Salvation Army-style furniture by cruising from street to street early on garbage days.

"That explains it!" Agnes said to herself as she concluded her analysis. She hadn't been dating Mr. Right *or* Mr. Clean. She had been dating Ebenezer Scrooge!

How could she possibly have thought of sharing a life—including a budget—with such a person? And what about children? Would Merle insist on dressing his future children in garage sale hand-me-downs?

Then Merle himself called—from work, of course. He had exciting news; his Aunt Sophia had given him her old house, which she was leaving for a retirement home. Merle needed some help "fixing it up a little" before he moved in.

Agnes couldn't believe that anyone would willingly move into Aunt Sophia's dilapidated home, even for free. She had seen the place, which hadn't been painted since the Depression. The bathtub had lion legs, the toilet had a pull-chain. The basement was cluttered from floor to ceiling with junk furniture, baskets of washed jelly jars, and stacks of moldy *National Geographic* magazines.

"What do you think I should do first to improve the house?" Merle asked eagerly.

Agnes didn't hesitate. "Torch it," she said, and hung up.

As Agnes resolutely pulled a folder of singles profiles from her cabinet, she knew what she would be looking for first: words like "generous" and "liberal", phrases like "money isn't everything," attitudes like "sharing and caring." She had, after all, learned some valuable tips.

### When in Doubt, Dump!

Gil the Gambler, Wanda the Workaholic, and Merle the Miser all have something in common. These three mate-prospects who were sensibly rejected by their partners are all, in a sense, addicts. They are much more interested in a *thing* (cards, work, money) that they ever could be in a *person*. Irene, Harold, and Agnes made wise decisions not even to consider a lifetime of playing second fiddle to an addiction, a "rival" that always wins. This kind of obsession is like a progressive disease which gets worse over time, never better. For example, miserliness usually spreads from stinginess with money to stinginess with affection, sex, conversation, and all the other forms of sharing that bind a marriage together.

Since Irene, Harold, and Agnes were seeking a stable, lasting marriage, they prudently took the long view in evaluating the rejects-to-be; they asked themselves what these unbalanced people would be like within the context of long-term *sharing*: the sharing of finances, of children, of time, of a whole lifestyle. This crucial question gave them the impetus they needed to make the correct decision: to move on.

Deciding on a mate resembles the process of considering an important, long-term investment. No sane investor want to stick with a high-risk stock which registers losses quarter after quarter. In the same way, *you should never settle for a mate about whom you have fundamental and rational reservations.*

Instead, return to the bottomless pool of more desirable potential mates and plunge back in! The diligent mate-seeker may encounter diversions, pitfalls, and wrong turns along the way. But the alert, persistent player *always* reaches the goal in the end.

# Chapter Ten

## THE DELIGHTFUL DILEMMA: THE PROBLEM OF PLENTY

### Maintaining Your Goals

In developing relationships with eligible candidates for a life partnership, your most difficult challenge is to maintain your original objectives in the face of a variety of choices. You don't want just a marriage ceremony; you want a fair, fulfilling life partnership. How can you guarantee that you will achieve this well-deserved experience for yourself? Perhaps the best way to answer that question is to reverse it and ask how you can guarantee that you will *never* obtain a relationship with an individual capable of giving and receiving mature love. There are four answers to this query:

1. Never undertake a serious, intelligent, systematic search for a suitable mate.
2. Remain in relationships such as those described in Chapter Eight which are degrading and manipulative almost from the onset of sexual involvement.
3. Keep exclusive commitments with partners who have late-surfacing neurotic obsessions such as those described in the previous chapter.
4. Settle for a basically nice individual who just hasn't finished

growing up in one or more important areas of adult development in the hope that with your nurturing example and instruction, he or she will ripen into someone worthy of your dedicated labor.

## Why "Raising" People Over the Age of 18 Doesn't Work

There are many men and women in our culture who are charming, decent, and presentable and who possess no serious, hidden or obvious vices. However, some individuals, for all their engaging, enjoyable qualities, just haven't made it past adolescence when it comes to dealing with life's many stresses, choices, and challenges. Because marriage involves ongoing interdependence as new situations are continually being confronted, it is crucial that both partners are capable of offering mutual support and good judgment when decisions are called for which will affect each of their lives.

When one person is incapable of adult responsibility in a given situation, his or her partner is saddled with extra burdens. A mature person in a relationship with one who is immature is bound to be frustrated. Frequently, the mature person seems like a parent figure and the immature partner rebels against any pressure to change. Immaturity can be couched in a number of personal styles. The following cases illustrate some common examples which spell disaster in a life situation.

## Sean's Reluctance to Marry Alice's Mommy and Daddy

Sean, in his six-month relationship with Alice Apronstrings, found himself growing more and more concerned with her incessant dependency on her parents, who lived in a nearby suburb. At first he had been pleased with what appeared to be a warm, supportive relationship between generations. He himself maintained close contact with his own parents in a distant city and considered a good relationship with parents an important asset to a future merger of two families by marriage.

However, he began to realize that Alice's relationship with her mother and father was quite different from his relationship with his parents. Alice consulted one or both parents on nearly every decision

106

she made. She spent an hour on the phone with her mother trying to decide whether to cut her hair into a full or partial shag. Each time she had her car serviced, her father insisted upon road-testing it himself before letting Alice drive it. Her mother had selected the color scheme and most of the furniture for Alice's apartment. Alice had admitted to Sean that she had a preference for vibrant colors but had capitulated to her mother's suggestion that muted earth tones were more tasteful. Whenever Alice left her office or apartment, she always "checked in" with her parents to let them know where she was going so they wouldn't worry.

When Sean realized that Alice was giving in to her parents' insistence that the young couple reconsider their plans to live in Sean's apartment after they were married, he decided that this was the last straw. Alice's parents were dismayed that Sean's residence was located in the city. The idea of Alice visiting Sean had never troubled them because they felt she was always safely escorted. However, the thought of Alice commuting alone by public transportation and living in an urban neighborhood was more than they could bear. "What about her safety?" they demanded to know, citing media headlines of muggings, rapes, and murders.

In discussing the issue with Alice, Sean sensibly pointed out that traffic accident statistics would indicate she was in more danger driving to work from her current suburban apartment than from possible violence on the city streets. Alice conceded he was right but pleaded with him to accept the alternative her parents offered rather than cause them worry and unrest. Alice's parents wanted to "help" the couple purchase a house in a "better neighborhood," not coincidentally less than a mile from their own home.

Sean realized that Alice had not severed her dependency upon her parents. They would hardly be content to stop interfering with future decisions he and Alice would make, should he accept their proposition. Alice's mother would most likely insist upon decorating this home as well. Next the parents would want to have a hand in selecting the young couple's social circle; they were already dropping hints about membership in a country club as a wedding gift.

Sean further understood it was not Alice's well-meaning but intrusive parents who were the problem, but Alice herself. It was more comforting for her to fall back on her role as a compliant child than to face making independent decisions and to take the consequences for mistakes. Marriage to Alice would mean marriage to three people—mother, father, and daughter—a bit more than Sean was willing to handle.

He discussed this at length with Alice, who was capable of admitting her overdependence upon her parents. Because she was the honest, caring person he had fallen in love with, she realized she shouldn't burden him with her immature attachments and guilt in a marriage. She honestly wanted to change. However, she had seen things from the perspective of a child for so long that they both knew her independence could not be achieved overnight.

Neither Sean nor Alice wanted to end the relationship without providing time for Alice to demonstrate her firm resolve to become independent and responsible within their relationship. They wisely decided to put wedding plans on hold and to give themselves at least another year before making a final commitment. Alice took the first step toward cutting her apronstrings by selecting a good professional counselor and beginning sessions *without* informing her parents of her decision.

## The Saga of the Lost Wallet

Georgia found that her prospective mate had problems too imbedded in his basic personality to risk working with. She had entertained high hopes that her relationship with Hysterical Hal was leading step by step to the altar. However, her aspirations were dashed one fateful day as the couple returned to the car after a shopping spree.

They had spent a wonderful weekend afternoon browsing in shops and boutiques, shared a leisurely lunch in an outdoor cafe, and listened to an excellent jazz concert by a trio of street musicians. Georgia deposited her newly-purchased treasures on the back seat and snuggled dreamily against Hal's shoulder as he reached into his pocket to retrieve his car keys.

Suddenly, she felt his six-foot frame stiffen and saw the color drain from his tanned complexion. Her first thought was that he was having an attack of some kind. She whispered urgently, "Hal, what's wrong?", as she readied herself for some dire medical emergency.

"It's gone!" shrieked Hal, his voice cracking.

"What, darling, what is it?" cried Georgia in bewilderment.

"My wallet! Oh my God, I don't believe it!"

Georgia stared open-mouthed in disbelief as Hal violently pounded the steering wheel before cupping his face in both hands, exclaiming forlornly in a muffled voice: "Damn it, it just can't be gone. Now what am I going to do?" he implored.

Georgia, still dumbfounded, stated lamely, "Maybe we should retrace our steps and try to determine if you left it in one of the shops, or whether it was stolen." She considered offering suggestions if the wallet had been stolen, such as changing his checking account, notifying his credit card companies, and obtaining a temporary driver's license, when she realized the absurdity of instructing a 32-year-old man on procedures for handling a missing wallet.

As she observed Hal, who was too busy cursing and bemoaning his fate to have the least interest in practical suggestions, she realized that she was functioning merely as an audience to his catastrophic reaction. Something about this huge, virile hulk of man, who prided himself on his athletic workouts and analytical thinking skills, falling apart when his wallet was missing struck her as tragically ridiculous.

It's not even as though he lost a lot of cash, she thought, remembering he only had ten dollars left in his billfold after their last purchase and, as a result, she had paid for lunch.

Georgia realized that, in months of dating, she had never seen Hal experience even a minor setback. With everything going his way, Hal was the picture of confidence, masterfully commanding both business and social situations. Yet even a minor and temporary loss of control sent him into a total freak-out. What would happen should he ever encounter a real problem? Georgia hesitated even to imagine such a situation.

As Hal continued to rant, now at her, for not paying enough attention to his feelings, she quietly checked her watch. Determining she had just enough time to catch the 3:30 bus, she said, "Hal, when you've calmed down, we need to have a talk about our relationship. Call me when you feel up to it."

On her way home she decided that reactivating and reorganizing her mate-search files would be far less complicated that trying to reorganize Hal's hysterical reactions to life's many minor inconveniences.

## Howard Declines the Role of Mentalist

Howard was discovering a similarly hopeless situation with his fiancee, Read-My-Mind Mindy, who had suddenly switched from her alluring, vivacious manner to a dour sulk.

"Now what's wrong?" he thought, realizing with some annoyance that Mindy's mood changes were becoming increasingly familiar. He could find no clues to explain her sudden anger. All he had done was to ask whether she had chosen a color scheme for the new furniture they were planning to order for their future lives together.

"Mindy, is something wrong?" he asked.

"What makes you think something is wrong?" sniffed Mindy petulantly.

Howard struggled to maintain his composure and find out what was behind Mindy's flare-ups. He felt he had to press the issue, though it was certain to lead to a confrontation. Distracting and pacifying Mindy for the last several weeks had only seemed to result in greater alienation instead of the trust he knew they should share at this stage of their relationship.

"Mindy," he said with concern, "we really need to put our dinner reservations on hold and have a serious talk. I'm not going to debate about the fact that something is bothering you. Your unexplainable hostility has been getting worse, not better, over the last couple of weeks. I need to know what is upsetting you."

After a long, sullen silence, Mindy blurted out, "If you weren't so insensitive, you'd *know* what's wrong!"

"Mindy," he said patiently, "if I don't know what is wrong, how can I be sensitive? I want and need to be sensitive to your feelings. Suppose you explain what they are and your reasons for them."

Mindy searched her purse for a tissue, and proceeded through angry sobs to construct a rather garbled scenario in which Howard had proven his insensitivity by insisting that practical concerns, such as new living room furnishings, were more important than sentimental expressions of love, such as a valuable engagement ring.

"Mindy, you're not being fair," he said in exasperation. "You're not the only one who's sentimental. I would have been more than happy to buy you an expensive diamond, and I told you so. I'm sorry I can't grant both of your requests. I'm not in that financial position. I left the choice up to you. You said you wanted the furniture first, and the ring on a future anniversary."

"I only said I wanted the furniture because I thought it would please you the most," Mindy said, glaring at him through mascara-streaked eyes. "If you had been paying attention to me, you would have seen that. Lately, all you've talked about is us, us, us. What about what *I* really want? You should have been able to tell how important that ring was to me, even if I was too polite to say so. Instead you get what *you* want. Can't you be more sensitive to *me*?"

Howard concluded he had indeed discovered indispensable information about Mindy. Beneath her attractive veneer, her talent and success, she was extremely insecure and self-centered. She expected a relationship in which her partner became her alter ego, a kind of magical father-figure who could know what she was thinking even when *she* didn't know, one who would pamper her hidden desires despite her superficial objections.

"Mindy, I'm not a psychic," Howard said finally. "I have to listen to what people *say* to learn what they want. Even if I could read minds, I wouldn't play your game. You want to sound mature and altruistic, but in reality you want to be spoiled and pampered. The irony is that I really wouldn't have regarded an expensive engagement ring as an extravagance—I said that and I mean it. I wanted you to have the gift which pleased you most. But you turned on me instead of taking responsibility for the choice you made."

Ignoring Howard's expression of legitimate concerns, Mindy took out her compact and began repairing her make-up. "For heaven's sake, darling," she said teasingly as she examined her face in the mirror, "we're already late for our dinner reservations. Why don't we just forget this whole silly misunderstanding and have a good time? I sometimes forget you men are used to having your own way, and I always get a little over-emotional when I'm ready to have my period."

For Mindy, the issue was closed along with her compact, and conveniently tucked into a mental category of sex differences and raging hormones instead of mature thinking.

Howard, however, had already decided to cancel both the dinner engagement and the wedding. It was clear to him that all the love in world could not make Mindy into a responsible individual within an intimate relationship. She had demonstrated she preferred using charm and silent storms to avoid confronting her own immature expectations.

Because Howard knew he needed a wife who could be fair, honest, and direct in their communication, he explained that the relationship would have to end. In this case, there was no conflict for Mindy. Ending a relationship only takes one.

### Esther Gives a Star-Gazer Infinite Space

Esther had also given up on Space-Cadet Spiro, and had all but forgotten him, only to find out three years later that time doesn't change for people who live in the "twilight zone" of immature expectations.

Shortly after her breakup with Spiro, a singer and songwriter, Esther had tried in vain to lay bets with her two best friends that he would convert the demise of the relationship into material for his next album.

"It'll be all about the tragic love of a man who needs space for personal growth and a woman who suffocates him with her need for intimacy," she had predicted. "In other words, it's bound to be a 'rock-schlock' hit."

Her friends, Rob and Barbara, a married couple Esther had known since college, refused to take the wager. They were sure she was right. Within a few months Esther had forgotten all about both her challenge and Spiro, as she found herself falling deeply in love with Dan.

Now she and Dan, her husband of two years, were sitting with Rob and Barbara in a kind of time warp as they all listened, amid hysterical laughter, as Rob played Spiro's latest album. Esther's half-joking prophecy made so long ago in her early days of dating Dan had indeed come true. Spiro had written a fairly popular song about the ultimate relationship that went wrong, not due to any mundane problem such as fear of intimacy, but because basic defects in the human condition made fulfillment between men and women impossible. The song with its plaintive lyrics seemed all the more comic to the four listeners because it assumed that the heroine felt the tragedy as keenly as did its hero.

Poetic refrains filled the room, describing a woman who was trapped in her world of strong feelings, pining for her lover's presence while he restlessly combed the skies for the meaning of the universe. However, the verses failed to move the present audience in expected ways as they attempted to control snorts, chortles and outright whoops of laughter.

Though she hadn't thought of Spiro in years, Esther found herself wondering at the fact that even though he "got his space," he could never be free. She had realized at the end of their relationship that Spiro had been in love with her image, one he had created and immortalized, and not her true self. She recalled how attracted to her he had been, yet how threatened. According to him, she was perfect—except for her need to "suffocate" him with too much intimacy and to control him through commitments.

Esther remembered the many times she had suggested their goals were not mutually compatible and that they should end the relationship. Many times she believed they had agreed to part as friends, only to find Spiro camped on her doorstep begging her to forgive him. On several occasions, this had been embarrassing because she had taken him at his word and invited another date for dinner. Each time Spiro won her back he would again start longing for "space" after several weeks of intimacy.

It finally dawned on Esther that Spiro wanted "all this and heaven, too"—for nothing. No honored commitments, no acknowledgment of legitimate heterosexual needs, no concern for a partner's goals or definitions of her own happiness. She had realized that Spiro resented her because she could love with all its risks, while he had to retreat as soon as he felt vulnerable. It was over for Esther when she saw that Spiro would use almost any manipulation to keep her involved with him, no matter how much it held her back from fulfilling her dreams. And all the while Spiro tried to convince himself it was the other way around.

113

Esther was brought back from her reverie by the song's clear refrain, which begged her to get in touch if she still believed they had a chance. Spiro wanted to express at last all the feelings locked inside for three long years.

Rob asked with mock seriousness, "So, Esther, are you inspired enough to leave Dan and blast off into space with Spiro?"

"You all used to talk about his flaky fellow when Esther and I were dating," said Dan, shaking his head. "But a song is definitely worth a thousand words. I think Esther's present condition may not be the turn-on Spiro is looking for," he continued as he slipped his arm around his very pregnant wife.

"Hear, hear, a toast to the eloquent earthling who speaks for all of us!" exclaimed Rob, holding up a slice of bread from his chicken salad sandwich. Like Marx Brothers characters, the four friends ceremoniously raised their bread slices and saluted each other before going on to discuss matters more relevant to their lives.

## Why Selecting a Mate Is Not Like Buying a Used Car

In the above cases, the mature partners maintained their goal of developing a fulfilling life partnership even if it meant postponing or withdrawing commitments leading to the ultimate investment of marriage. In most cases, as these three out of four sample situations indicate, it's best to *trade-in* before becoming involved in a relationship based upon *trade-offs*. Emotional investments are completely different from material investments because they depend upon assets and credibility within the human character.

It's not quite fair to say that the best things in life are free. If you've gone to the considerable trouble of becoming a grown-up person capable of sharing intimacy, you have avoided a lot of short cuts to become what you are. You belong with someone who has done a similar amount of work in this area. Regardless of whether or not your financial situation requires you to accept a variety of trade-offs in economic goods and services, if you've developed your own emotional assets, you have no reason to settle for "lemons" and "clunkers" in the arena of love.

## *Avoiding Deficit Relationships*

While it's important to keep a high level of self-esteem in all of your relationships—with family, friends, and co-workers—it is especially important in intimate heterosexual relationships. A seductive temptation is to believe it is easier to put up with another's immaturity than to accept the pain of cutting ties and moving on.

Once you've given in to your fears, it's easy to find rationalizations for "clutching" rather than continuing your search for a truly suitable mate. You don't have to look very far to find these excuses. Regardless of which one you might be tempted to select, they all boil down to the same thing: you shouldn't expect mature fulfillment because you don't deserve it.

Some convenient self-denigrating sources are easily found in he following areas:

1. *Self-defeating myths:* there aren't enough suitable partners out there, anything is better than nothing, or all human beings including yourself are basically losers, this is the best you're ever going to find.
2. *Childhood experiences:* you don't deserve anything good, just remember all the faults your parents found. If your parents failed to convince you that you are unworthy to receive fulfillment, your immature partner, as the above cases illustrate, will be happy to supply deprecating labels which should convince you that you have no right to expect high standards when you're such a low-life yourself.

Some common accusations from immature partners are: you aren't understanding enough; you're insensitive; and/or you're suffocating and demanding. The variations are only as finite as the derogatory terms in the English language (and perhaps other languages, if your immature partner is multilingual).

## *Determining Whether Criticism Is Constructive or Manipulative*

It's very important to keep your self-regard, and to make an honest assessment of the charges within the context of the situation. If they are true, you have to ask yourself what you are doing in *any* relationship. Pull out gracefully, and work on yourself before continuing your search for a mate.

You have to be particularly alert to this possibility if you have become seriously involved with a string of "losers." Without realizing it, you may be selecting problem-people who enable you to act out some negative self-fulfilling prophecy or unresolved anger toward the opposite sex. Feeling victimized, rejected, and bitter while searching relentlessly for a mate is actually a thin disguise for permanently avoiding intimacy.

If you find yourself having thoughts like: "All men are exploitative, they only want one thing"; or "All women are gold-diggers, they just want to take you to the cleaners," you are ignoring your own propensity for selecting people with these negative character traits, or the possibility that you are misinterpreting the attitudes of others.

This kind of emotional baggage will make finding mature love impossible, and make hurting yourself and others highly likely. In this situation you need to invest your valuable time, energy and money into psychotherapy, not dating.

If, on the other hand, the accusations of your partner are unfair, you must wonder about the level of love your partner claims to have for you when he or she attempts to mask personal problems by diverting the blame to you. Occasional disagreements are par for the course in any relationship, but cheap shots and impulsive behavior don't belong in any adult interaction, least of all one in which you entrust your emotional life.

If you continue an immature relationship (and all it takes is one partner to make it that way), you will become involved in a tit-for-tat contest of love-hate exchanges and power plays. Besides being childish and destructive, these relationships are highly unstable and therefore quite susceptible to collapse under stress and change.

116

Such "deficit" relationships require partners to maintain a delicate balance of emotional attacks upon one another to remain stable. If one partner scores too high, the underdog will raise the ante. Needless to say, continual one-upmanship is inevitable. Besides being volatile, such relationships don't leave much room for the development of love, trust, mutual support or efficient strategies in dealing with life's many problems.

If you desire marital fulfillment, then a good relationship which is moving toward that goal is better for you than being single. On the other hand, being single and uninvolved is preferable *by far* to an unstable, immature relationship.

# Chapter Eleven

## THE ULTIMATE COMPATIBILITY: MUTUAL LOVE GOALS AND LIFE GOALS

*Integrating Love With Life*

In the previous chapters, you have read numerous case studies alerting you to vices or immaturity in a prospective partner. In these situations, you need to run, not walk, back to your mate-search files in order to begin anew. However, when you've found a good, responsible person capable and desirous of a commitment, how can you be sure that this is really "it"?

You and your partner are now at a very challenging point in your relationship because all future decisions you make together will affect your lives and those of your friends and family. You have each ascertained that you are decent, fair, loving individuals with no investment in hurting others. You are very attracted to one another; you may have begun to love each other deeply. Before formalizing your commitment and going public with engagement announcements, you need to give yourselves time to consider the last level of compatibility necessary for a fulfilling life.

In our complex society, individuals who love each other often have very different ideas about what this means. They have different methods of expressing love as well as different expectations about what

119

the person they love should give them. Most of us know cases in which these individual differences are easily worked out among both couples and friends. However, we probably can cite other examples in which relationships become strained or ruptured by irreconcilable misunderstanding between two very decent individuals.

When a good marriage is your goal, it is risky to think that individual differences in approaches to life can always be reconciled by the saving grace of "true love". It is also worth the effort to try to predict patterns which will lead to compatibility in all important aspects of marriage.

## Your Goal Is a Model Marriage—But Which Model?

When you are satisfied that you have found a suitable potential mate, it is a good idea to review your answers to the 20 questions answered in Chapter Four, especially the last half which involve lifestyle preferences and expectations. In integrating sexual love and marital expectations with the rest of your life, it is important to avoid compromising your basic values if they are incompatible with those of your partner.

In reviewing your answers to questions 11-20, pay particular attention to your attitudes about questions 13 and 20. Consider your past answers to these questions in light of your present relationship:

13. What are my feelings about heterosexual intimacy? Do I want mutual self-disclosure and the sharing of deep feelings to occur frequently, occasionally, or rarely in my marriage? Do I want to have sex with my mate frequently, occasionally or rarely? Do I want affection and devotion—verbally and behaviorally expressed frequently, occasionally or rarely?

20. How much time do I expect my mate to allow me for pursuing my own separate endeavors? How much time do I intend to allow my mate? Are my expectations for my mate and myself identical, fairly similar, or significantly different? What is my rationale for my position?

These two questions are "loaded" because the answers are very subjective. For example, two people might answer "frequently" to each part of question 13. However, if you discussed their responses with them in more depth you might find vast differences in their interpretations of the word.

## Sexual Love—Different Strokes for Different Folks

Bert and Alicia believed they needed a great deal of sex in marriage. Over the course of their relationship they discovered that Bert interpreted this to mean approximately twice a week, while Alicia had something closer to twice a day in mind.

Another couple, Maurice and Clare, found they agreed upon the quantitative but not the qualitative expression of sex. He preferred long, sensitive, romantic interludes which, however, left her somewhat bored. In the case of Lorraine and Todd, similar incompatibilities emerged because her passion and intensity unsettled him. He had not envisioned a mate who could be so "animalistic."

Emotional and physical needs expressed in sexual love are basic to each individual's identity as well as a couple's concept of their relationship. Fulfillment depends upon compatibility, not compromise. You and your mate need to be very honest with each other. Are *you* really fulfilled? Are you really meeting *your partner's* needs in sexual expression? Many situations can be salvaged with greater awareness and understanding. Often partners are willing to change in the direction of more passion and tenderness once they discuss more exciting alternatives. Education, reputable books on sexual love, or pre-marital counseling can be helpful in these cases.

Sometimes, however, individuals may be satisfied with their attitudes in this area and understandably unwilling to change. Bert and Alicia, for example, did not feel it would be fair to one another to try to compromise. After honestly discussing their different needs for sexual frequency, they felt that no alternative could be satisfactory. Alicia really wanted a mate who could express the same kind of sexual intensity she felt each time they made love. Bert wanted a passionate mate, but one who enjoyed a balance of other activities along with their intimate relations. He found sharing music and poetry as stimulating as sex. Alicia was frustrated because she viewed these experiences as foreplay to passionate lovemaking. Ending many of their evenings together with Yeats and a tender kiss was more than she could bear. Both Bert and Alicia were right about sex and love—but not right for each other.

## Differences in Approaches to Life and Marriage

When most people use the term "a good marriage," they rarely stop to consider that more than one "good" approach to marriage is possible in our open society. They also overlook the fact that good approaches to marriage may not only be different but also incompatible. Sexual needs are different among mature individuals. Needs for emotional intimacy and priorities in marital values are also different.

For many individuals, achievement needs are paramount. Yet they may have a desire and capacity for a marital relationship as well as a strong emotional investment in their careers. While these individuals prefer that work comes first, they can be counted upon by their spouse and family in important situations. Because their lives are influenced heavily by work, these persons may schedule their activities carefully to insure they give quality time to those they love. If you want to marry a person of this type, you must be able to accept your partner's passion for achievement without seeing it as competing with your love life or family life.

Individuals who identify strongly with their vocations appreciate marital love primarily for the emotional support which inspires them to even greater levels of creative or intellectual accomplishment. They like to share their area of interest with their spouse and will often select mates in similar or complementary fields of endeavor. Couples with these priorities develop approaches to marriage which are mutually supportive of their work, either within separate careers or within a situation in which one partner promotes or assists the other's career.

## *Making the Family a Mutual Enterprise*

Some people, regardless of their career interests or job competence, envision a marriage in which family life is the most important component of the couple's identity. These individuals are very involved with the mechanisms necessary for a smoothly running household and quality family experiences. They derive the greatest satisfaction from activities which highlight family interaction such as participation in games, educational enrichment, sports, holiday celebrations, trips, and gatherings with other relatives. They may also enjoy community involvement, which makes them feel they are improving their immediate environment as well as promoting their family image.

These individuals want a marital lifestyle oriented around health, child development, and social improvement. Orthodonture and the PTA are more frequent topics of conversation than career concerns or their own intellectual endeavors. For couples with these priorities, both their love needs and achievement needs come together in an ambition to attain and promote a loving, dependable marriage and a happy, healthy family.

## *Romance and Ambiance In Marriage*

Some individuals envision a marriage in which their special relationship receives the highest priority. They need to carve out a space for being "in love," despite the demands of careers and family. They are reassured by all sorts of sentimental symbols which make them feel unique and cherished.

Romantically inclined individuals like their loved one to give them highly personalized gifts, attention, and time. While they can be counted upon in all areas of career and family life, they need private shared experiences as a couple away from children, relatives, friends, job demands, and civic duties.

They are highly demonstrative in their expressions of affection and use of endearments. Hand-holding, candlelight dinners, love notes, weekend getaways, and sentimental mementos give them the greatest fulfillment whether they have been married for one year or fifteen. They may be hard-working in their careers and excellent parents, but they identify most strongly with being the special individual who is loved by Mr. or Ms. Right.

Some individuals have a deep capacity and need for a very direct expression of love, stripped of all its social roles. They need to feel emotionally connected with all people and relate in any interaction with intensity, compassion, and great appreciation for the ironies of life. They are fairly oblivious to what people do, and far more concerned about what people are as individuals. Whether sophisticated or homespun, this type of person is always trying to cut through differences in social values and relate to something more basic in others.

In a marriage they are most "at home" with a kindred spirit because they can fully express themselves without social protocols. Their sensitivity and loyalty to those they love insures their responsibility in work and family life, but they do not identify with their professional role, the role of a husband or wife or the role of a parent.

They seek special time together with their partner but do not feel as dependent upon romantic trappings as the type described above because deep intimacy is so much a part of their basic make-up. As parents they are empathic and responsive to the individual needs of their children without emphasizing the family as a unit. The kind of marriage they want depends upon sharing trust and love without limits with a mate, and fostering the development of the unique qualities of each family member.

## Possibilities and Impossibilities of Compromise

Despite the current woeful tomes about the decline of the importance of the family, we perhaps have more opportunity for compatible marriages today than at any other time. For example, traditional models of marriage often fit nicely into unrealistic stereotypes—with males as skillful achievers and females as more emotional and dependent, each sex supposedly compensated by vicariously living through the aptitudes of the other. Women were supposed to ensnare reluctant males into marriage, "the tender trap," even though survey studies have consistently shown most men to be happiest when they are married.

Compromise had to be the name of the traditional marriage model or serious power struggles were likely to ensue. If compromise did not result in sufficient fulfillment for one or both partners, or if dramatic life changes, such as the celebrated mid-life crisis or retirement, catapulted couples into a different relational framework, marriages could become considerably strained.

Social changes have had a strong liberating effect upon married people, encouraging them to be individuals who are true to themselves within a marriage rather than a socially-prescribed half of an institutionalized duo. However, more choices in marital roles also places more responsibility upon couples who are considering a life partnership. Couples need to explore together their feelings about sexual and emotional intimacy, as well as their ideas about marriage, family and overall approaches to life, *before marriage.*

All approaches to marriage can change unpredictably in rare situations or under extreme circumstances. However, when couples begin with similar values and expectations, they are usually better able to form a foundation for trust and understanding which makes compromise workable rather than oppressive.

In looking over the approaches to marriage described above, it is easy to see that some combine more easily than others. When you explore individual differences with your prospective life partner, realize that when one person's fundamental identity is compromised by the relationship, it is not something that can be "worked on." *People cannot be what they cannot see.*

In other words, if individuals with one perspective simply can't grasp another perspective, then try as they may, they won't be able to perform by those standards no matter how much they love their partner. Coming to terms with this fact of life and love does not have to be an adversarial process. You may feel justified in being angry with prospective partners who have concealed vices or immaturity (perhaps even from themselves). However, a loving person of good character with a different approach to sex, love, and married life is no more at fault for honestly living up to his or her ideals than you would be for doing likewise.

Obviously, the ideal situation is for couples to share the same concept of marriage. However, common perspectives seem to occur between individuals primarily concerned with career and family accomplishment, and between those most concerned with the romantic quality of the relationship.

Individuals oriented primarily towards career, and those identifying primarily with their family unit, are similar because they focus more upon the role they enact in a group than upon their special feelings as a couple. These two types of individuals place similar emphasis upon role identification rather than personal relationships. Compromise is necessary in priorities involving career aspirations and family activities, but this diplomacy is not difficult when there is a great deal of mutual respect for each partner's life approach.

Similarly, individuals who need a very romantic marriage and those who need deep intimacy are not so far apart in their focus upon the quality of the personal relationship. The partner concerned with intense intimacy may feel somewhat awkward about the romantic trappings involved in expressing love, while the partner concerned with romance might feel somewhat unsettled with a high degree of emotional candor. However, the former partner is sensitive enough to enter into the love-play expected by a romantic mate, while the latter is able to be open and empathic with a mate focused upon emotional intensity.

Mixed approaches to love and life are most likely to cause strain when one partner orients marriage around a career or family enterprise while the other sees marriage primarily in terms of the quality of the relationship itself. The partner identifying with the romantic quality or intensity in the marriage has a hard time accepting the idea of being "penciled in" for love between career activities such as board meetings or professional conferences. In a relationship organized around family activities, these individuals lament that they never go anywhere together without children, relatives, friends, or social contacts. Yet, partners who see marriage as an important component in their career or family identity regard their behavior as a very practical approach to love and life.

### Perry and Ramona Find That "Never the Twain Shall Meet"

Ramona and Perry's relationship illustrates a common example of "oil and water." Ramona realized she was chronically complaining to Perry that their relationship lacked spontaneous romantic gestures. After a particularly tearful interlude, she arrived home from work the next day to find a beautiful bouquet of roses and a poem extolling her importance in Perry's life.

Needless to say, she was touched and elated. However, the next month on exactly the same date she again received a bouquet identical to the first with a similar note attached. In following months, the same phenomenon repeated itself like clockwork. Her suspicions aroused, Ramona telephoned the florist and found, not surprisingly, that her busy fiance had arranged an account to provide monthly tributes of his appreciation for her. The special feature of this package deal was the "poem of the month" dedicated to the recipient of the flowers. So much for Perry's conversion to romance!

A philosophical sort, Ramona knew that Perry really did love her, was reliable and responsible, and attended as best he could to her emotional needs. However, his style showed little awareness of the kind of loving gestures she truly craved.

She didn't want to be angry or critical. But it was painful and frustrating to suppress the highly developed romantic dimension of her personality simply because Perry could not understand it. Perry gave her a devoted form of love which was meaningful to him—but sadly lacking for her.

Ramona knew she must either compromise or end the relationship. She opted for ending it gracefully, rather than resenting someone she loved and admired who simply was philosophically and emotionally incapable of understanding or meeting her fundamental expectations in love.

### When You Are Both Right, Are You Right for Each Other?

In considering ultimate levels of compatibility, give yourself and your partner time to reflect upon each other's values and expectations in marriage. Romance is only socially sanctioned in the early stages of courtship and marriage in this culture. After that, couples are on their own. Some individuals tend to focus upon romance only in these early stages, regarding true marital love as mutual support for "higher" goals in either the public or domestic sphere. Some extend love play and sentimental private ceremonies into their "golden years." To some, the early stages of romantic involvement are a springboard to unlimited depths of understanding and intimacy.

You need to understand what the next stages of your courtship will mean to you personally and to your partner. If you find your goals for emotional fulfillment are simply incompatible, it is imperative to face that fact and be honest about it at this stage, before you involve others in your relationship.

It may be painful and disappointing for each of you to find your "good catch" isn't quite right for you. But if you have begun to love this person, you will want him or her to be truly happy. If you love yourself, you will also want this experience. You can't compromise your basic emotional identity and be fulfilled. Moreover, it would be tragic to resent a fine individual or to be resented yourself for simply being what you are, or because your approaches are too dissimilar to meet each other's needs in love over the long haul.

In this situation, you need to reassure each other that you are each on the right track. You have found a decent, mature partner who viewed you in the same loving way. With the knowledge that you have each reinforced the other's value as a person, you should be able to let go and to continue your search with renewed confidence.

If, on the other hand, you find in your exploration of ultimate compatibility that you are in close agreement with each other regarding marital fulfillment, or that you can easily work out unfettered compromises in basic love/life approaches, you've tapped into the "mother lode." As individuals and as a couple, you know what love and marital life mean to you. You are secure in the knowledge that you can emotionally support one another. You have more to give than before to your family, friends, and co-workers as you "go public" with your commitment of love.

## *Ron and Ingrid Find Slices of Life a Piece of Cake*

Our compatible couple Ingrid and Ron are discovering this beautiful experience with one another in the most mundane of all circumstances. Let's look at another vignette of their lives as they continue to pull even closer together despite the complexities of developing a life partnership. We find them together at the end of a dismal day in Ingrid's life. Her geriatric automobile had earlier suffered its version of cardiac arrest during rush hour traffic on her way to work and had given up the ghost in the middle of an intersection. Yet, curled upon the couch next to Ron in the apartment they now share, she could only marvel at the fact that she could be so happy with him and wretched about the ordeal she was relating, all at the same time.

Her ears were still ringing from the insults of outraged drivers, and the banter of her smart-mouthed high school students when they learned of her plight after she arrived late and dirty from trying to push her old heap out of the way of oncoming traffic.

Yet she soaked up Ron's compassion, his helpful suggestion for managing until she could replace the car, and his gentle humor as she related the last of her students' jokes about her car, she couldn't get over how lucky she was. "Even when I'm utterly miserable, I'm happy because you care," she blurted out, confusing herself with the apparent contradiction.

As Ron slipped his arm around her in understanding, she suddenly found herself uncharacteristically bursting into tears and letting down a guard she did not even realize she had. "You know, I didn't even know this myself," she said shakily to Ron, "but it's been harder than I've let on to drive that old heap while I dutifully paid back my student loans. Not everyone treated me seriously because I had to drive a car like that, and now I'll have to go out and replace it with something not much better. But you've always appreciated me for what I am, not what I have."

"Not hard to do," said Ron, stroking her face tenderly, somewhat in awe of her painful self-disclosure. From the first date, he had seen Ingrid's shield of bravado about her difficult, economically restricted lifestyle. He was touched that she trusted him enough to share her deeper emotions with him.

He recalled how she had made it possible for him to face his own feelings of inadequacy over meeting his clients' needs in a system of never-ending cutbacks in social services. He credited her with helping him avoid burn-out as he struggled to provide aid to the families in his case load. With her emotional support, he had found the additional strength to return to graduate school at night to prepare for a position he had wanted for a long time but had postponed in order to organize his life and assist his daughter's readjustment following his divorce.

"It just keeps getting better for us, doesn't it?" murmured Ingrid into his shoulder, as if reading his thoughts. Ron, who for a moment had a fleeting overview of just how much they had given one another and what a lifetime of these exchanges could mean, managed to answer, "Yes," before yielding to feelings for her which could never be expressed in words.

# Chapter Twelve

## MAKING A COMMITMENT: SMOOTH SAILING OR CHOPPY WATERS?

### *Make a Victory Bonfire*

Now that you and your partner have found each other and started making plans for sharing a life together, it's time for a few final touches.

If you haven't already done so, contact the various singles clubs you joined and de-activate your file. Then collect all the profiles and letters you received and dispose of them. For this symbolic step, you may want to splurge on a bottle of champagne and invite your friends who have cheered you on through the dating process. They will get a kick out of the celebration and, if still single, they will take heart from your success story.

You will probably want to raise an appreciative farewell toast to your memories of the interesting people who were not-quite-right for you. Make a wish for their eventual success in love. But above all, congratulate yourself on your present good fortune. You've earned it!

### *Going Out of Circulation*

How do you reply to date-seekers who haven't yet gotten the message that you're no longer looking? A brief, kind note informing them of your ineligibility is best. You might add a P.S. encouraging them to persevere and wishing them the kind of happiness you now enjoy.

## Going Public

You and your partner have shared a substantial amount of time alone, developing your intimacy. Now it's time to tell others of your commitment. Tell your families, your friends, your co-workers. Place an announcement in the local newspaper, if that's your style, or shout it from the housetops. You're proud of your partner, after all, and you're both brimming over with happiness. Make it official. Tell the other people who are important to you.

As you move out of the initial, "desert island" phase of your relationship and enter the social world together, you'll probably have a merry time getting to know each other's friends and relatives. You'll also be laying the foundations for a lifetime together as you form these new ties. In addition, the experience of seeing your partner within the total social context of his or her life provides you with an eleventh-hour opportunity to confirm your commitment, or to change your mind.

## Patrick Takes His Children to the Orthodontist

When Gina started getting involved with Patrick's friends and family, she liked what she saw of his behavior toward them. Although Patrick was a non-custodial parent, he saw a great deal of his two children. He did all the usual recreational things with them—bowling, playing video games, going fishing—but Gina was particularly impressed with his active involvement in their schoolwork and other important areas of their well-being. He attended parent-teacher conferences, helped the children with their math over the phone, and even checked out library books to foster their budding interest in astronomy.

Compared to Gina's very absent ex-husband Dan, who breezed through her children's life once a year and barely knew what grade they were in, Patrick was a revelation. She loved his capacity for caring and responsibility, and was delighted by Patrick's voluntary assumption of some of the more boring but essential duties of parenthood, such as taking the children for their check-ups. When he asked her playfully one night why she loved him, Gina replied, "Because you take your kids to the orthodontist!"

Knowing Patrick within the context of his family life—and of hers—reinforced Gina's decision to marry him. She correctly perceived that the caring and responsibility he showed to his children would have a positive effect in other important relationships as well.

### *Kate Mends Her Father's Jacket*

When Chet began participating more completely in Kate's life, he was particularly pleased with her touching concern for Al, her widowed father. She invited him for dinner every Sunday, and together they worked on the newspaper crossword puzzle, one of his favorite hobbies. Before he returned home, Kate would sew on any loose buttons on his clothes and do other mending he brought to her.

Once when Chet observed her sewing Al's jacket while she chatted with him about his pet canaries, he thought anew what a lucky fellow he was to have found such a thoughtful woman for his wife.

Kate had been thinking of Chet with similar appreciation. He had spent the previous weekend performing carpentry work for his mother so that she might get a better price on the old house she was trying to sell before moving to Florida.

Kate and Chet had shown each other that they valued the people with whom they had spent their past. Would they not also value the partner and the children with whom they would be spending their future? Both felt greater confidence in their choice of a mate.

### *You've Got to Have Friends*

There are three important social areas of a person's life: work, family, and friends. Because marriage is ideally a special kind of friendship, your partner should have a good "track record" in his or her friendships. After all, friendships are "chosen family"; they reflect what we are, where we've been, and how we wish to continue our lives.

We all know that a person who has *no* friends, like Scrooge in *A Christmas Carol*, is flashing one of the worst possible signs of poor mental health. Similarly, a person who has only the most superficial types of friends (drinking buddies, for example, or shopping-spree pals) should not be considered a good prospect for an intimate, lifetime relationship. But a person who has cultivated a circle of close, long-term, mutually supportive friendships is usually an excellent bet.

When Sid and Marlene found that the fifth reunion of their respective college classes was coming up, they decided to attend both. The experience produced a dramatic affirmation of what they had each fondly believed about the other.

Sid learned that Marlene had kept in touch with her best friends from college, some of whom lived in their town, and that they all had only glowing remarks to make about her. They could always count on Marlene to "come through" when they were in a jam. Sid's friends made similar comments to Marlene about him: that he had been the only "real grown-up" in the whole fraternity, and that he had gone on to fulfill his early promise as a responsible adult.

In effect Sid and Marlene received an endorsement from their long-time friends. Moreover, they found that for the most part they liked each other's friends. They seemed to be decent, caring, and sensible as well as a lot of fun—like Sid and Marlene themselves. In fact, the final validation of each other from their friends convinced the couple to move up their wedding date. Why wait when all the evidence was in that they indeed had a good thing going?

As you enter your partner's sphere of work, family, and friends, you should above all watch for a confirmation of two main qualities: *caring* and *responsibility*. If these qualities are lacking, you also know what to do next: congratulate yourself on having found out in the nick of time, breathe a deep sigh of relief, and resume dating.

Nora, for example, received an unpleasant surprise when she visited Van's office.

## Nora Hails a Taxi

When they were alone, Van seemed to Nora an unusually caring and sensitive man. However, a very different picture emerged when she visited the office which he headed. Employees cringed and stammered as he swept past. When Van left Nora to bark orders at a terrified computer operator, she took the opportunity to accept a cup of coffee from his secretary and chat. She noticed that the secretary chewed constantly on antacid tablets.

When Nora asked her sympathetically about having an upset stomach, the secretary blurted, "Oh, it's my ulcers—they always seem to act up when Ivan the Terrible—Mr. Vanderhorn, I mean—comes in." Nora probed a little further and found that one of her desk drawers was a veritable medicine chest of drugstore remedies she had to keep on hand for herself and the other employees.

"I guess we're a nervous bunch," the secretary admitted as she noticed Van advancing toward her desk.

Nora had heard enough. If Van was such a tyrant over his employees, what kind of a bully would he become as a husband or father? It was a sobering, though helpful, revelation. Nora thanked the secretary for the coffee and told Van she was taking a taxi home.

"Suddenly I have an upset stomach," she explained.

Nora wisely did not wait for Van to drive her to ulcers, but ended the relationship that night. She knew a person who abuses power in one set of relationships would most likely abuse it in others. The brief trip to Van's office had probably saved her years of unhappiness.

Remember: *When in doubt, bail out!*

## The More I See You, the More I Love You

One chief characteristic of a great marriage is pleasant surprises. We don't mean bringing home a bouquet of flowers or baking a special cake, as nice as such conventional gestures sometimes are, but rather a pattern of spontaneous *acts of thoughtfulness* on the part of both mates. This pattern should also characterize the lives of a committed couple planning marriage.

135

## Tony Has a Brainstorm

When Tony called Danielle to invite her and her five-year-old daughter, Stacey, for dinner at his house, Danielle thought that they were going to enjoy another of his fabulous Italian meals. Instead, she discovered that Tony had not been out of town on business for the past two days, as Danielle had been told, but busy preparing a surprise for Stacey. Stacey had shown some reluctance to move into Tony's house, as the family-to-be planned to do after the wedding, so Tony had decided she needed something to make the move more appealing. He had purchased a pink canopy bed—the bed of any little girl's dreams— and refurbished a private bathroom just for her. Stacey squealed with delight. Danielle was deeply moved by Tony's extraordinary sensitivity to the child's feeling. Tony enjoyed all the hugs from "his girls." He had been well-paid for his efforts, and made light of his project to Danielle later, when they were alone.

"My motives were purely selfish," he said. "I figured if Stacey had an irresistible bedroom and her own bathroom, you and I would have more undisturbed time together at night in *our* bedroom!"

## Judy to the Rescue!

Sam found a surprise of a different kind waiting for him when he returned from a camping trip with his son's Boy Scout troop. They had had to stay an extra day, snowed-in by a freak April storm with not a phone for miles. Sam knew Judy would hear the weather report and understand they would be late returning, but he was worried about his parents. His mother was an invalid, his father was recovering from a recent operation, and Saturday was the day he always did their shopping and picked up their prescriptions. What if they had run out of something important? He need not have worried. As soon as Judy realized Sam was snowbound in the mountains, she drove over to his parents' house and attended to their needs. When Sam was finally able to call them and learned of her surprise errand of mercy, he was both relieved and delighted. As he joked appreciatively when he made his next call to Judy: "I knew I was engaged to Wonder Woman, but I didn't know you doubled as Florence Nightingale!"

## Harry and Elise Find Two Surprises Are Better Than One

Harry and Elise surprised each other one Sunday morning. Elise tiptoed out early, leaving her partner asleep. He was dead tired from a long business trip. She walked to the local stationery store and photocopied important legal papers that Harry would need for an early Monday appointment; it would save him the hassle of an extra stop in the rush hour. When she returned home, Elise was surprised to find Harry working at his computer, surrounded by spread-sheets. She supposed he must be trying to calculate his income tax. But Harry had concocted a surprise of his own. "Guess what?" he exclaimed happily. "According to these budget projections of our combined incomes, you can go to college full-time next year and finish your degree. You won't have to keep that crummy part-time job!" Genuinely touched, Elise could only manage to say, "Wow! What a guy!"

## The Best Declaration of Love

What do all these surprises have in common? They indicate deep empathy for the partner, and an awareness of his or her needs, concerns, and general well-being. They also indicate an attitude of creative problem-solving toward the little difficulties of merging lives. Partners who respond to each other's needs with such meaningful, helpful surprises are making a profound declaration of love. Surprises of this kind are also evidence of an ever-new, ever-deepening relationship, one which will never stop growing. The renewable gift of a little imagination and thoughtfulness is the most solid, as well as the most romantic, basis for marriage. If you find this theme running throughout your engagement, you will certainly find it after the wedding, too.

## "Break Up or Move In": If, When, How, and Why

As your relationship progresses, you will probably want to start living together. (That is, *if* you have no children! If you do have children residing with you, it is often wiser—for all sorts of legal, conventional, and psychological reasons—*not* to live with your partner until after the wedding.) These days most couples contemplating marriage do share a home before marching down the aisle; it's the romantic and the economical thing to do, of course, but also the best possible "practice" for the daily interactions that marriage will involve.

Since you have both been clear from your first date that your final goal is *wedded* happiness, this trial period before the actual wedding should be relatively short, perhaps a few months or a year. Long-term cohabitation without marriage is usually unwise for both parties.

Most important, this "trial marriage" is your last opportunity to determine if the lifetime relationship you both have in mind is workable or unworkable.

In short, living together is the ultimate test of a couple's true compatibility in many crucial areas. If you find your love blossoming (instead of wilting) as you share time and space, you're truly ready to apply for a marriage license.

*Equality* in all things will be your guideline at this point. How could you wish anything less for someone you love, or for yourself? Equality in the practical aspects of sharing a home, such as handling money and chores, is vital. If you experience either of the following "warning signal" situations, it's time to beat a hasty retreat from the altar.

## Theo Liberates Himself from Franny the Freeloader

Theo's relationship with his vivacious girlfriend Franny seemed to be progressing as smoothly as he had hoped when he first moved in—until the first of the month rolled around and she presented him with a stack of bills. Theo certainly intended to pay half of the rent and utilities, but he was shocked when Franny stubbornly declined making any contribution whatsoever. "It's the man's job to pay the bills, isn't it?" she asked coolly.

138

"What century are you living in?" Theo retorted, baffled. "Did you get stuck in a time-warp?" He went on to point out that her salary was larger than his; to expect half their shared expenses from her bank account was only reasonable. "And what's this overdue charge item for a $200 snakeskin purse from last August?" he continued angrily. "Am I supposed to pay that, too? I hadn't even met you in August!"

Clearly, Theo didn't know Franny the Freeloader as well as he thought he did when he made the mistake of accepting her offer to move in. However, he knew very well what to do now. He packed his suitcase and left Franny holding his first-and-last check for *half* a month's expenses.

Theo had learned the hard way that working out an equitable financial arrangement is an essential detail that needs to be completed *before* sharing a home. A viable relationship should be *victimless*. Franny's selfish and antiquated ideas about billpaying made Theo a victim, not an equal partner.

### *Debbie Tells Alvin Allmine What He Can Do With His House*

When Debbie decided to accept Alvin Allmine's proposal that she move into his house, she had misgivings from day one. First of all, he made it quite clear he expected her to pay half the expenses. This would have been fair if he had not been a prosperous stockbroker, with inherited wealth besides, and she had not been a struggling dental student. She had hoped he would gallantly accept the lion's share of the expenses, especially since the upkeep on his townhouse was much greater than that of her small apartment. But Debbie dipped into her savings and plunged into the living experiment, figuring she could carry the burden for a while.

But the arrangement didn't even make it through the week. Debbie was familiar with Alvin's possessive attitude towards money, but she wasn't ready for his idea of sharing time and space. When Debbie asked where she could hang her clothes, he reluctantly cleared a slot in one of his many overflowing closets. When Debbie asked which of the three bathrooms she could use to keep her cosmetics in, Alvin began automatically to say, "They're all mine,"—but caught himself and grudgingly allotted her a few shelves of one bathroom. He used the other two for steaming his collection of tropical ferns, and for storing photography equipment; Debbie was asked to stay out of both.

By this time, Debbie was beginning to feel like Little Orphan Annie. But she thought things could only get better. Wouldn't they?

Feeling lonely one evening, Debbie suggested they send out for a large pizza and split it. "Let's order two small ones instead," Alvin responded. "I want one to be all mine."

Debbie had gotten the picture. "You can have both," she said decisively. "*I'm* splitting!"

Alvin looked thunderstruck. "But what about sharing the house?" he asked.

Debbie called back over her shoulder as she slammed the door: "Stuff it. It's *all yours!*"

Fortunately for Debbie, it only took a few days to discover she was living with an unusually tall two-year-old. At this age children are unable to share anything willingly with others: they want *all* the toys, *all* of Mommy's attention. When they are forced to share, they usually throw a temper tantrum or go into a sulk. As Debbie wanted a *real* child some day (not one of the deep-voiced, bearded variety), she was wise to leave Alvin Allmine clutching his playthings and to return to the adult world.

## Ron and Ingrid Move In and Move On

Ron and Ingrid had been living together since they celebrated their "Interdependence Day" four months before, and had decided to move to a larger apartment than the ones they rented as singles. They chose a place with enough room for weekend visits from Ron's daughter Donna and for the baby they hoped to have in a year or two.

With the help of good friends, they moved in and started collaborating on building more furniture to match the bookcases which had been their first joint project. Ingrid was now more proficient with hammer and nails, thanks to Ron's patience. Ron's cooking repertoire had expanded to include some of her Danish specialties.

Now they performed calisthenics together on the floor as they waited for their combined families and friends to arrive for a little house-warming-and-engagement party. As they counted sit-ups, they glanced around with pleasure at the paintings they had selected and framed themselves. Already they could look back fondly on little domestic achievements characterized by cooperation, consideration, and mutual respect. Together they were happier people than they had been apart.

Listening for the doorbell to ring, they reflected that it would be a lovely evening; they had already built a loving life. They looked forward joyfully to their wedding, of course, but in the highest sense, Ron and Ingrid were now a happily married couple.

# Chapter Thirteen

## GETTING ENGAGED:
## THE VALUE OF PRE-NUPTIAL CONTRACTS

### *Economic Realities and Future Forecasts*

Passion can be stable and ongoing when augmented by some real "nuts and bolts" planning and preparation. As you bask in the happiness of your new life together with a vast future ready to unfold before you, it's a good idea to turn some of your energy to important practical concerns. Economics has always been a "hard core" reality in any marital situation.

Cinderella and Prince Charming, for example, lived happily ever after at the expense of hordes of peasants and military legions in a castle provided by Charming's daddy. The average modern couple has to take more than a few cuts in this romantic life-style. Moreover, unless your economic situation is one in which you can afford to be oblivious to the crass concerns of material holdings (and even if so, your parents or older children will be scrutinizing the effects of a marital union upon inheritance), you will need to make these issues a joint concern.

Therefore, as you make your wedding plans, along with the appointments with ministers, food caterers, and florists, you should also schedule joint appointments with your respective attorneys and accountants. You need to obtain information about the laws in your state regarding changes in your economic status which will occur following a marriage.

## Obvious and Obscure Legal Ramifications of Marriage

In your meetings with legal advisers, you will need to handle a number of straightforward issues such as reviewing your previous wills and making appropriate revisions where applicable. In addition, it is also good planning to begin considering more subtle implications of the effects of marriage upon your financial holdings. For example, in cases in which couples are older and have children, or those whose parents might need health care, marital implications can become quite complex.

Many previously married couples have complicated divorce agreements which may be affected by remarriage, or they may have future responsibilities which are not apparent in their present life-style, such as college costs when children are older. Partners with inherited assets or complicated wills may have legal stipulations regarding marriage, especially second marriages. You each need to make a full disclosure of all debts and assets to each other. In addition, you should review all documents pertinent to these issues with each other in the presence of appropriate consultants.

## When Existing Marital Laws Best Serve Couples' Needs

Couples with few personal assets or debts, those who are marrying for the first time or who have had uncomplicated, childless divorces, or who have suffered the death of a spouse with no other heirs, tend to find that most state laws adequately protect their interests. Laws governing marriage generally assume joint ownership of all property and assets couples amass together. (Some states, however, still retain discriminatory attitudes toward women in these areas, which are well worth investigating and attempting to correct through pre-nuptial agreements.) If your situation seems to be adequately covered by your state or county laws, there is little value in incurring the expense of a private contract covering death or divorce in your relationship.

## The Value of Pre-Nuptial Agreements

Many couples with more complicated situations find that marriage laws, which vary considerably according to location, are not always adequate to protect their special circumstances in the case of death or dissolution of the marriage. Other couples may want a clear, specific agreement between themselves to stave off the concerns of children of former marriages, or of parents who want their grandchildren to be sole beneficiaries in the event that a new marriage would jeopardize previous intentions.

While you don't want to become obsessed with planning for dismal possibilities such as the death of a spouse or divorce (particularly the latter, which is remote if you've chosen each other wisely), you do need to feel protected in the event of "worst-case" scenarios.

Many couples are afraid to test their relationship with official awareness and acknowledgment of the full legal implications of their marital contract. However, a positive approach to these matters should make you trust each other all the more for exploring these issues and developing alternatives which might be more fair to each of you than laws made according to customs which may not be compatible with your present life-styles.

If mere revisions and modifications of documents over which you have full control (such as wills) do not appear adequate to your specific needs, you may want to consider developing a pre-nuptial contract satisfactory to both of your situations. Costs for pre-nuptial contracts should not be excessive if you have your ideas well worked out in writing before consulting your attorneys. To save time and money, you may decide upon having one partner's attorney draft the agreement and then have the other partner's attorney review it before final drafts and signing.

145

## Problems with Pre-Nuptial Contracts

We should warn you that there are drawbacks to this practice which need to be considered. The first, and easiest to overcome, is the fact that not all people who have composed these documents in the past were particularly rational or mature in their marital expectations. Thus, a number of precedents in divorce cases have made the courts wary of individually designed contracts. One can well understand judicial sentiment when reviewing examples of this quasi-legal genre.

In considering your own contract, you will want to stay as far away as possible from all forms of silliness and exploitation. Clauses citing requirements for personal behavior as grounds for maintaining the marital contract should definitely be avoided. Idiosyncratic obsessions with issues such as who empties the garbage or how fat a spouse becomes in the future, for example, do not belong in a serious pre-nuptial agreement. If you and your partner consider the possibility of an individually designed contract, we would hope that considerations of these types are the farthest things from your minds—or you will probably not have long to wait to test the effectiveness of your agreement (which will no doubt be thrown out) following the end of your marriage.

The other main problem is that even when a contract is clear, fair to both parties and reasonable, existing laws generally take precedence over individually designed contracts in contested cases (though a well-stated pre-nuptial agreement may be used to guide court decisions). However, when couples start out creating an environment which is fair and rational, the odds are much greater that they will maintain this environment in times of stress.

A pre-nuptial agreement (if you decide upon this option) should emphasize greater *fairness* than the laws may provide. It should also remove the potential of financial blackmail in a marriage. When one partner's socio-economic position is legally weakened by entering into a marital contract, you want, as a couple, to try to redress this wrong.

If one partner should want in the future to break the marriage contract, he or she should not feel compelled to remain trapped in an unhappy relationship because the other partner will unfairly lose hard-

146

earned assets, or even worse, seriously jeopardize elderly parents' or children's futures. For example, some states have marital laws which may discriminate against women with personal assets.

However, both sexes risk exploitation when their special circumstances are not easily addressed by existing laws. In these situations pre-nuptial contracts can officially acknowledge these potentially oppressive conditions and officially declare a joint commitment to fairer terms. In that spirit, even if a marriage later begins to flounder, if the legally stronger partner does not contest, the weaker partner can either leave with what he or she was rightfully entitled to, or stay—without feeling blackmailed—to work out the difficulties.

## *Jerry and Nicole Tailor a Pre-Nuptial Contract to Meet Complicated Issues*

Jerry and Nicole's situation exemplifies complicated legal ramifications which might be better addressed by an individualized agreement. Each had been previously married and each had two children. Nicole's were still dependent but away at college. Jerry's were in their early teenage years. Nicole lived in a large house which she and her former husband had bought from Nicole's mother, who had since passed away.

Although the house was now in her name and fully paid for, most of the furnishings, comprised of many valuable antiques, had been willed jointly to Nicole and to her sister and brother. It had been recommended to the beneficiaries that they hold onto these articles for some years in order to realize the full appreciation value. Because Nicole's two siblings were in somewhat transient situations, they had elected to let her continue to enjoy the use of these articles until their sale.

Jerry had recently become owner of a co-op apartment. He also owned the home of his former marriage. However, this house was targeted as an investment to be sold off to pay for his children's college education.

Nicole wanted to share the title to her home with Jerry, which would enable them to have both a city and country residence. Yet, she wanted to be sure that the antique furnishings, partially her brother's and sister's inheritance, were protected. Jerry wanted to share ownership of his co-op apartment, in which he resided with Nicole. However, he wanted to retain sole title to his house, the investment for his children's education.

The couple decided to draw up a pre-nuptial agreement in which each relinquished joint ownership to any house which was not used as a joint domicile. To be sure that Jerry's co-ownership of Nicole's house did not confuse pre-existing agreements about its contents, Nicole and her siblings made up an itemized list of all furnishings inherited from their mother and a contract for their sale at a specified date. This agreement among beneficiaries was cited in the pre-nuptial contract, which also specified that Jerry made no claims upon these articles in the estate.

Jerry and Nicole's agreement was designed to protect each of their interests and to allay any concerns on the part of their respective families that the new spouse would obtain investments intended for others.

## *Let Common Sense and Professional Advisers Be Your Guide*

In cases in which couples try to modify existing laws to suit their special circumstances, an environment of reason and thoughtful exploration of alternatives should prevail. If you or your partner begin to feel pressured or emotionally intimidated, negotiations should cease until this problem is resolved.

This is especially important if one partner is urging conditions which are not considered advisable by the other's attorney. Couples should adhere closely to the advice they receive from their legal consultants and steer clear of do-it-yourself approaches, which could be ineffective at best and unfair to one or both partners at worst.

Couples who are able to begin their lives together in the spirit of fair expectations and full disclosure of their economic and legal obligations may feel sure that they are gaining emotionally in every way from this investment of time.

With these practical details carefully nailed down, it's now time to turn your attention to resolving any problems with adult relatives or children who might object to your marriage. If these obstacles don't apply, you are one of the fortunate couples who can skip the next two chapters and joyfully begin to plan for your marriage ceremony.

# Chapter Fourteen

## RESOLVING SPECIAL PROBLEMS: PARENTS AND OTHERS

While you have been clearing any legal or financial obstacles out of the way, it's possible that another type of obstacle has arisen within your family: people who object to your marriage. This type of obstacle is, unfortunately, more emotionally trying than legal paperwork, but the good news is that such problems have solutions, too.

One of the most common objections couples encounter from their families has to do with differences in religion, race, or social background.

### *Eleanor and Alex Set the Date*

When Eleanor started dating Alex, her parents became uneasy. From their point of view, Alex was unthinkable as a future son-in-law in every respect; he was a Russian-American, practiced the wrong religion, and completely lacked the "eastern Establishment" social credentials they valued. "He's not one of us," they warned Eleanor.

Eleanor had enough confidence and insight to realize she wasn't dating Alex only to annoy her parents. From her point of view, Alex had everything she desired in a man—he was kind, stable in character, ambitious, sexy, and endlessly interesting. Moreover, Eleanor and Alex *enjoyed* each other's cultural differences. They could swap stories for

151

hours about their "worlds apart" childhoods and feel all the closer for it. In no way did they consider their differences an impediment to their relationship but, rather, a special dimension of it.

As the couple drew nearer to making marriage plans, Alex's parents and all the couple's mutual friends offered enthusiastic congratulations—but the attitude of Eleanor's parents dipped from cool to Arctic. "No one that we know will accept him," they admonished Eleanor. "And what about the children?" Finally, they refused to attend the wedding.

At first Eleanor and Alex were distraught. They hadn't wanted to hurt anyone, after all, and had hoped the hostile attitude of Eleanor's parents would disappear as they got to know Alex better. However, when it became painfully apparent that they could not perceive Alex as an individual, and a worthy one at that, Eleanor got angry. "It's *my* choice and *my* life—not yours," she told her parents. "If you can't respect that reality, it's your loss."

Eleanor's parents tried every trick in the book to manipulate her into calling off the wedding. They sent her grandmother to talk to her, her mother feigned illness, her father stormed about rewriting his will. Eleanor disliked having to deal with their soap opera antics, but she and Alex held firm about the date for the wedding. It was a painful and upsetting couple of months for both partners, but they felt their love had been strengthened by the rejection.

"I hope your parents grow up some day," Alex concluded philosophically. "Until then, let's just let them know from time to time that the door is always open, and get on with our lives. That's all we can do."

## Avoiding Emotional Blackmail

If you find yourself confronting parents who try to blackmail you emotionally, *don't* succumb. Such reactions are never expressions of concern for your welfare, but manifestations of a profound, selfish insistence that you repeat the pattern of their lives, live according to their standards. Be kind, of course: try to make it clear that you're not rejecting *them*, but only their inflexible ideas. As a mature adult in a free society, you have the right to expect that your family will respect your lifestyle and your choice of a mate. If they do not, try to maintain contact and proceed with your wedding plans. Most families do become more accepting with time. And if they don't, you now have a new family to love, the one you and your mate are about to found.

## A Different Hurdle: Impossible Relatives

You might encounter a different kind of problem before the wedding as you are getting to know each other's family—the problem of impossible relatives. The subject of many "in-law" jokes, these individuals usually come in one of two varieties: the terminally boring and the just plain dangerous. Whatever their type, they all exhibit one common characteristic, the inability to practice socially acceptable levels of self-control in one huge area of behavior. Your task is to *impose limits* on them. (Skip trying to reform them. Their families have already tried for years and failed.)

## Robert Applies the Techniques of "Case-Management" to His Boring Future Father-in-Law

When Robert first met Miriam's father, he had been forewarned that Virgil's verbal diarrhea could bore even the most stout-hearted listener. However, Miriam's description of his output failed to do justice to the reality. Virgil buttonholed Robert, sat him down, and babbled at him in excruciating detail about a ham radio he had built some decades ago. When he finally departed, Robert told Miriam frankly, "I love you, dear, and I accept your family, but if I have to see Virgil every week, I'll go bananas!"

Miriam understood, having suffered through Virgil's ham radio talks frequently as a child. She assured Robert that Virgil could only bear to tear himself away from his basement workshop for visits twice yearly. Robert perked up a bit, but the thought of having Virgil as a houseguest for even an occasional weekend still appalled him.

Miriam reminded Robert of his career in administration at a mental hospital. "What do you people do with a difficult patient at work?" she prompted.

That's easy," Robert replied. "We have a meeting and apply suitable restrictions to the case."

"That's exactly how everyone in my family handles Dad," Miriam encouraged him. "Now let's determine how to get through a two-day dose of Virgil the Verbose. Our first precaution must be to eliminate any opportunity for him to get you into an armchair. He's deadly with a captive audience."

Robert suggested that the best plan might be to save considerable yard chores for Virgil's visits. Because Virgil rarely noticed if others listened, Robert could enjoy some outdoor exercise, tune out, and fantasize as the older man followed him around, jabbering happily of condensers, receivers, and antennae.

The plan worked splendidly on Virgil's next visit; he went back home pleased, Robert and Miriam retained their sanity, and their well-tended yard was the envy of the neighbors.

This couple solved their case-management problem by *setting limits* and *planning distractions*, just as parents do with small children. But what about a relative who is not so harmless or docile? In this instance, use the methods of *animal-taming* instead.

### Clarice Draws the Line With Her Delinquent Future Brother-in-Law

When Clarice first heard about Sol's highly disturbed brother, she was aghast. The black sheep of the family, Bobby had been dishonorably discharged from the Army for brawling, had served time in jail for assault, and frequently ended a visit home by "accidentally" smashing some breakable object his relatives particularly prized. Clarice correctly perceived it could be dangerous to associate with Bobby at close quarters; this hot-tempered, hard-drinking, middle-aged delinquent had a clear history of violence. When she learned that Bobby had actually slapped his sister on a recent visit to her house, Clarice made up her mind.

154

"I know you care about Bobby and you'd like to help him," she told Sol, "but I don't intend to become one of his 'accidents.' What are we going to do when he visits this town?"

"Well, it's usually a mistake to let him into the house," Sol reflected, "so how about meeting him at a crowded restaurant?"

"Good idea," Clarice agreed. "And make it a restaurant with no bar."

When Clarice finally met Bobby under the restricted conditions on which she and Sol had decided, he was perfectly charming. Kept sober and subdued by his surroundings, Bobby presented no trouble at all. "I could even enjoy his company," Clarice commented afterwards, but added hastily: "Once in a while, that is!"

Clarice and Sol were able to solve the problem of occasional socializing with a potentially dangerous relative by the tactics of "safety in numbers," by meeting him only in public. This strategy also produced the unexpected bonus of reducing Bobby's usual number of visits per year; he grew bored with Sol and Clarice, since they provided him with no opportunity to play his neurotic game of breaking things and baiting people.

If you have an impossible relative of the dangerous variety, approach the problem with the same caution you would use in dealing with a wild animal. Don't take chances: see him or her only under circumstances that guarantee prior de-fanging and de-clawing.

When handling impossible relatives of any kind, always *plan ahead* for your own protection. Don't let them abuse you. Outwit them!

## A Special Note for Special People—Widows and Widowers

Widows and widowers cope with their bereavements in a tremendous variety of ways. They also differ widely in the ways they experience re-entry into dating and marriage-bound relationship. In some cases, the two processes are intricately related. If you are a widow or widower or about to marry someone who is, you have probably noticed one of the three most common kinds of reactions to the dead spouse: *deification, posthumous divorce,* or *normal grief.* The first two often can pose a mild problem.

155

## Nelson Stops Feeling Guilty

Even after Nelson's late wife Edna had been dead for two years and he had formed a deeply satisfying relationship with Michelle, he still felt guilty about Edna's long, painful last illness. "If only I had made her quit smoking sooner," he would say, "it might have saved her." Unreasonably, he blamed himself. In addition, he extolled Edna's many virtues at every opportunity.

"There will never be another Edna," he would say tearfully.

Finally, Nelson's adult daughter took him aside and said, "Dad, it's all right to mourn for Mom, to miss her, and to remember her appreciatively. But you shouldn't *worship* her!"

Fortunately for Nelson—and for Michelle—he listened. Nelson had unconsciously deified his late wife, doing no good to her or to himself while possibly jeopardizing his relationship to his patient wife-to-be.

"Mom would want you to be happy," his daughter urged. "Let her rest in peace now and enjoy your life with Michelle."

It didn't take Nelson long to follow this sound advice. Within a month, he and Michelle were dancing happily at their wedding—and there were no reproachful ghosts standing in the wings.

## Rita Releases the Past

When Rita recovered from the sudden shock of her husband Elmer's fatal heart attack, she was surprised how wonderful she felt. "Guess what?" she would ask when she called her married children. "I don't have to watch your father's dumb TV shows any more!" Or, on another occasion, "Guess what? I went square-dancing at the church. I'd forgotten how much fun it is!"

In short, Rita was the classic "merry widow." It had taken Elmer's death to make her realize what a dull, narrow, isolated life his stodgy habits had imposed upon them. Her children were delighted that she was finally going out and having a great time.

Rita recognized that she was, in effect, *divorcing* Elmer beyond the grave as she probably should have done in his lifetime, long ago. She didn't grieve deeply since the relationship had been dead years before Elmer expired.

Rita enjoyed her bright new life even more when she became engaged to Ilan, a lively Israeli widower. However, as she settled into the security of this new relationship, so different from her life with Elmer, the contrast troubled her. "I flushed twenty-seven years of my life down the drain with him," she complained angrily.

Ilan took a positive approach. "Maybe so," he soothed her, "but you have kids who love you, you have me, we've got our health and a little money, and you're not yet even fifty! Let's kick up our heels!"

Rita realized he was making sense. "Guess what?" she said to Ilan. "No man could ever have a more *appreciative* wife than you're going to have!"

Ilan smiled. The dark memories of Elmer had been dissipated by laughter—and the "merry widow" was ready to change her status to that of a happy bride.

## *Normal Grief Heals with Normal Living*

Unlike Nelson and Rita, who encountered a hitch in the usual grieving process, most widowed people go through a brief period of intense sadness, followed gradually by a renewed interest in living—and loving. If you or the widowed partner you have found happen to hit one of the stumbling blocks outlined here and a little sensible advice doesn't clear away the difficulty, you might want to consider short-term grief therapy with a qualified professional.

Whether or not your first marriage was entirely happy, you are certainly entitled to a happy marriage now and you don't want to blow it. Cherish what there is to cherish in your past, of course, but go on to your new partnership with the brightest prospects for success.

# Chapter Fifteen

## DELICATE SITUATIONS: ADJUSTMENT PROBLEMS WITH CHILDREN

### *New Family Relationships with Children*

One of the most common problems in this age of remarriage involves adjustments when one or both partners have children by a former spouse. These situations require considerably more effort than those involving parents or other relatives of an engaged couple. Techniques such as those described earlier in the chapter for managing difficult relatives are not appropriate for younger children because of the deep emotional bond children need to maintain with parents in order to develop their individual capacities. Even when children live in the ex-spouse's household, the importance of this bond remains undiminished.

Regardless of any future relationships parents might form, their children will always have some dependence upon both their natural mother and their natural father. Therefore, a workable relationship with a former spouse based upon mutual concern for the children is always in a child's best interest. When partners share children with a former spouse, it is crucial for them to accept this situation, and to create a space for children to grow within the framework of the new relationship without dissolving important and necessary ties with their past.

If you or your prospective mate are parents, you are in a situation in which becoming a mature person yourself and selecting a mature partner truly pays off. Insecurity and self-centered expectations can create disaster for all concerned, disaster which continues into the next generation through the lives of damaged children.

You can avoid the heartache, which all too often occurs in some remarriages, by being responsible enough to realize that parents obviously cannot forsake their children, and just as obviously cannot sever all contact with the mothers or fathers of their children. On the other hand, a marital relationship cannot become subordinate to a former family relationship, to unnaturally prolonged emotional ties to a former mate, or to serious conflicts which have not been worked out before undertaking remarriage.

## *Resolving Former Marital Conflicts Before Starting a New Life Together*

Whenever possible, problems with former spouses should be resolved *before* entering into a new marriage. Some problems, such as an ex-spouse's influences upon the children that may be too subtle to control directly, will be discussed later. However, there are basic issues which may need to be tightened up to avoid intrusions by a former spouse into the new marriage.

For example, if a partner has a history of problems with an ex-spouse over visitation schedules, support, or intrusions upon his or her privacy, it is very important to investigate alternatives to bring the situation under control. Brainstorming together, talking with other divorced people, or consulting with psychological or legal professionals may be helpful in solving minor difficulties. The following case is an example of a painful and exasperating problem with an ex-spouse which was easily rectified by a well-designed behavior modification program.

160

## *Rosa Uses a "Silencer" When Gunning Down Clyde*

Rosa had become so used to Clyde barging into her home two hours late on visitation days, using her telephone to make "urgent" business calls, and criticizing her in front of the children that the possibility of better alternatives didn't occur to her.

She had resigned herself to spending every Saturday morning with children whining "Where's Daddy?" every three minutes, or "Why can't I go to the park with Joey? There's nothing to do around here until Daddy comes." These incessant complaints were then capped by Daddy's belated arrival, his snide remarks, and further restlessness on the part of the children as Clyde bellowed: "Keep the children quiet! I have to make important telephone calls."

Clifford, her intended, knew that something needed to be done for both her mental health and his own. "We'd better use our brains," he said. "Otherwise I'll be sorely tempted to use my brawn on your obnoxious ex, which would be the last thing the children need."

As the two began throwing out ideas about possible alternatives, Rosa discovered that the solution was really simple when her creativity was not stifled, as it had been in the past, by an infantile mate. Realizing that she had gradually learned to feel helpless by Clyde's constant petty intimidation, she enjoyed a surge of exhilaration as she found her problem-solving faculties returning.

Before the next weekend visit, she telephoned her ex-husband and told him she had enrolled the children in a local library program and that he could pick them up there. In this new situation, the children were stimulated by books and films as they waited for their dad. Moreover, Rosa, who had situated herself close to the receptionist's desk, could enjoy quiet, solitude, and safety as she perused her favorite literature.

When Clyde made his predictable grand entrance at noon instead of the scheduled ten o'clock, there was no captive audience to greet him. His characteristically atrocious behavior was completely stymied by the surrounding environment.

"It was so funny," Rosa told Clifford later. "Out of sheer habit, Clyde came blustering through the door and shouted the first syllable of my name before turning beet red as the librarian cast her icy stare upon him. All he could do was come over and whisper, 'Where are the children?' He started to criticize me for not supervising them well enough, but I quickly put my finger to my lips and nodded to the librarian, who was still eyeing him warily. I pointed to the children's section. All he could do was meekly go retrieve them and leave as I smiled and waved good-bye.''

## Stronger Social Sanctions: An Emotional and Financial Investment

Unfortunately, many situations are not nearly this simple. When an ex-spouse acts in more threatening ways, or when issues involve breaches of the financial terms of the divorce contract, legal intervention may be necessary. Negotiations with an ex-spouse (moderated by attorneys or family systems professionals) may be helpful. However, when these strategies are inadequate, court action may be necessary.

When a partner enters into litigation with an ex-spouse, considerable strain is placed upon the new relationship. In these cases, couples may need to plan engagement periods which take the slow processes of the justice system into consideration. Partners also need to provide mutual support as they clear the final obstacles to a new life together.

A partner involved in litigation needs both encouragement and understanding. However, the investment is well worth the undertaking to both partners if it eliminates soap opera scenarios which can be quite dangerous emotionally, financially, and sometimes even physically to a new couple and the children they share.

## Being Accepted by a New Family: What to Expect

Marriages in which one or both partners are parents differ *significantly* from childless unions because the environment created from the onset must provide emotional support for *both* the adult couple and the children from former marriages who share this new bond. If your prospective marriage is one of the many today which falls within this category, you may already have discovered a very hard fact: while you can replace a defunct former marriage with a fresh start with the right mate, your children or your partner's children often have trouble replacing their old family with this new one.

As much as you love your prospective husband or wife, and as much as you would like to give your children and step-children an instant "happy family" to make up for the pain and loss caused by divorce, you can't expect them to accept a step-parent in the same manner as a natural parent. However, over time, step-children may develop relationships with step-parents which are as deep or even deeper than relationships with natural parents (although these relationships will be qualitatively different, unless children are very young when the new marriage is formed).

## Some Problem Prevention Techniques for Prospective Step-Parents

If you are going to become a step-parent, your safest initial role with your partner's children is similar to one of a close, loving, responsive aunt, uncle, or family friend—until the children themselves initiate a relationship which permits more parental involvement. Cues for direct parenting can take years unless the children are very young. In some cases, children may never initiate a parental relationship with a step-parent, but the relationship may be very close and valuable to both parties in its own right.

## Who Can Discipline Johnny?

Because your prospective marriage cannot confer automatic parent-hood, a number of potentially serious problems are avoided by leaving discipline in the hands of the natural parent. Only when children have developed a long-term, trusting relationship in all other areas is it wise even to broach this level of involvement. Unfortunately, even when your parental style is highly similar to that of your partner's, your intrusion into the role of parent by acting as disciplinarian may be regarded as threatening by your step-children.

Without trust and security cultivated by a long-term relationship with you, your step-children may not be emotionally ready to accept your authority as a parent. Your best strategy for insuring good parenting of your step-children is to be encouraging and supportive of your partner's parental approaches. It is helpful to natural parents when supportive partners provide opportunities for them to vent their frustrations and sort out concerns and conflicts regarding their children by discussing options and alternatives.

By becoming a sympathetic and insightful listener in these private discussions, rather than playing the co-disciplinarian when your partner is having problems with his or her children, you help your mate stay in touch with his or her own strengths. At the same time, you have avoided the costly mistake of forcing yourself into an unnatural role with step-children in an attempt to back your partner up with your own authority. Your display of respect for your partner in front of his or her children will also convey your approval of your partner's judgment and competence in all areas, including discipline.

## When the Natural Parent and the Step-Parent Disagree on Child-Rearing

Differences in values and approaches to child-rearing are best settled between the two adult partners *in private*. Disagreements in front of the children should be avoided at all costs. However, if you as prospective step-parent disagree with some of the approaches your partner is taking with the children, be sure to find out *why* he or she is adopting these methods.

Your initial disagreements may lessen when you understand more about the intricacies of the children's special needs, or about conflicts your step-children may be experiencing of which you were unaware. If you have basic respect for each other's competence as individuals, you should be able to reach an understanding which is in the best interest of the children and which transcends any petty criticisms.

## *Never Try to Usurp the Natural Parent's Values*

Step-parents should also make it a rule never to pressure partners into accepting their methods for child-rearing over those of the natural parents. If disagreements are serious, however, even after thorough discussions of respective positions, the natural and prospective step-parent may want to consider consultation with outside resources which provide information about effective parenting skills.

For example, you may want to start by contacting community mental health organizations for recommended publications on general approaches to parenting, or, more specifically, request information focusing upon children's adjustment to a new marriage. You may decide that you need more specialized and personalized assistance with your situation and seek counseling or therapy with a professional specifically trained in child development and family relationships.

These options can enable you and your partner to become more sensitive to each other's parental values and provide a framework for negotiating dissimilarities in approaches. If philosophical differences are not too serious, you can work together to develop strategies which are healthy for both your prospective marital relationship and the children who will share in this bond.

## *Serious Value Conflicts: Back to the Philosophy Date*

If you continue to disagree in important areas which affect decisions about children's health, education, and welfare, you may have to do some serious soul-searching about the advisability of continuing this relationship. You may recall that in the very earliest stages of your relationship we advised you to provide opportunities for a "philosophy date" in order to determine your compatibilities in value systems.

While this approach is highly effective in initially screening out basic incompatibilities, deeper core beliefs frequently don't surface in couples until they reach the stage of "going public". As the partners make formal commitments involving interaction with each other's families, they may uncover differences in standards not apparent in more abstract discussions of values.

This situation is particularly true in philosophies involving child-rearing because in our society standards for adults are different from those for children.

## Either/Or Situations for Parents

Parents who are reasonably convinced that their child-rearing values are safe, sound, and effective may find it necessary to take a strong stand behind their beliefs, sometimes at the cost of the relationship. If you as a parent have exhausted all possibilities for a satisfactory mutual agreement between you and your partner over child-rearing approaches, you have a right and obligation to resist interventions which you do not believe are in your children's best interest.

No matter how deeply you may have become emotionally involved with your prospective mate, it may be necessary to break your commitments and terminate the relationship in order to protect your children, your rightful authority in raising them, and the integrity of your own beliefs.

This a painful prospect, but you are preventing much greater pain and damage to your children and yourself by maintaining your well-tested system.

If you hold firm and continue to navigate by a reliable compass rather than one you don't trust, you preserve your existing contract with your children and honor your responsibility to them. One of our basic premises in the process of mate-selection is that *no new marriage can be successfully built upon irresponsibility*. This is particularly true in the case of dependent children.

By upholding your responsibilities while facing heartbreak and disappointment, you enhance your self-esteem and maintain your credibility as a parent. You haven't succumbed to the spell of false hopes. You have also left yourself open to experience the right relationship for you rather than a dream which could only turn into a nightmare.

## *Focus on Trust, Not Authority, When Stepping into Step-Parenthood*

Step-parents who share basic philosophies about raising children with natural parents still face a number of challenges in developing relationships with children. As a prospective step-parent, you will have the greatest success in developing a close bond with your step-children if you enter the relationship much as your partner, the natural parent, did when the children were born.

Natural parents develop trust with their infant children (long before discipline enters into the picture) by responding to their needs with love, sensitivity, and concern. Similarly, as a prospective step-parent, you can become alert to many areas of the children's lives which could be facilitated by your helpful gestures.

Whether your partner's children are small and impressionable, or tower over you and are hip to things you've never heard of and would rather not know, they have many legitimate needs. Neither tots nor teenagers can get too much appreciation or attention in constructive areas of development from mature adults.

The techniques for initiating a close relationship change with age, but a child's need to feel highly regarded by adult relatives remains the same. You don't have to smother them with gifts and surprises like a perennial Santa Claus. In fact, because you can't buy love, creating such an artificial environment would actually be a serious obstacle to the development of a trusting relationship.

However, you can become aware of your step-children as individuals by becoming attuned to their interests, talents, goals and challenges as they navigate the choppy waters of growing up. For example, when you force yourself to sit in rapt attention while an eight-year-old butchers Bach at a piano recital, or smile between clenched teeth as a sixteen-year-old shares the latest heavy metal rock sensation with you at a deafening decibel level, you are demonstrating a sincere willingness to relate on an intimate basis.

By caring about what is important to the child rather than expecting devotion and acquiescence to your needs, you define your role as a concerned adult who can be relied upon in all the important areas of life. When an adult relates with a child in this way over time, it becomes difficult for an outside observer to tell whether this adult is the "real" parent or the step-parent. At this stage of an adult/child relationship, it also becomes difficult for the two participants to make this distinction because it has become meaningless.

## Pre-Nuptial Tips for Natural Parents

Our main recommendations for natural parents is to maintain a strong parental role and decline the temptation to abdicate the most unpleasant responsibility of all—discipline—to the new step-parent. It is more helpful to provide a forum for positive initial interactions as your partner enters into the process of becoming a step-parent.

You know your children far better than your partner and you are their best advocate. Your partner, the step-parent, needs your assistance and encouragement in his or her initial attempts at forging a lifetime relationship with your children. As you maintain a strong, visible parental role which will keep your children secure and allay possible fears that you will discard them for this new relationship, you can simultaneously make suggestions regarding the little day-to-day needs your children have which your partner can meet.

Your partner's responses to a myriad of mundane events such as chauffeuring your youngster to Little League practice, or helping with a homework problem, will gradually create interdependencies which form the basis of deep relationships. The more the two of you can support each other in a calm, nurturing environment during your engagement period, the easier it will be for children to adjust to the new family relationships.

## Tailoring Wedding Plans to Avoid Conflict with Children

Children have critical transitional periods at different points in their lives due to social norms which pressure them, sometimes suddenly, to change their goals and behavior. It is generally a good idea to set a wedding date which does not conflict with these emotionally-charged periods in a child's life.

For example, you may want to reconsider a summer or fall wedding date if you have a youngster who is preparing to start school for the first time. If your last dependent child is a junior or senior in high school, you may want to begin married life after he or she goes off to college, rather than to begin the enormous task of family adjustment with an adolescent who is preparing to leave home.

If you and your prospective mate began your relationship shortly after a divorce, it is important whenever possible to allow a mourning and transition period for your children.

Unless they are very young, children generally need about two years to heal from the stress of divorce. Of course, this consideration must be weighed against other factors, such as economic or social pressures, which may produce more stress by the couple living separately for this period of time.

You should avoid wedding dates which fall within the same period as an important ceremony in your child's life. Children like to be the center of attention of the extended family when they partake in some type of initiation rite such as a Bar Mitzvah, a First Communion, or graduation from high school or college. You want to be careful not to preempt their "big day" with your own wedding.

If remarriage involves changes for children in households, school systems or a major relocation to another town or city, you need to strongly consider these issues before making wedding plans. You want to make the transition as easy as possible by familiarizing the children with their new situation before making abrupt relocations.

By giving yourselves a long enough engagement period, you can schedule trips, visits, and activities which involve the children in their new surroundings. You and the children will feel much more in control of your circumstances if you have the household plans, child-care, schools and community activities set up in your new situation before your wedding day.

It's important to make your children's futures in their new surroundings seem as concrete to them as possible. It's particularly and educational opportunities in the surrounding areas of your future home are both practical and symbolic ways in which you can maximize your children's sense of security when facing change.

## Addressing Separation Problems in Relocation Situations

If relocation means moving from the home town of a natural parent, you will have to make great efforts to reduce the impact of separation upon the children. You may want to negotiate changes in visitation agreements to improve opportunities for children to see their natural parent.

You can also encourage frequent contacts by telephone and letters. Taking advantage of modern technologies, such as tapes and videos which can be easily mailed, is also a way to keep natural parents more visibly involved in their children's lives. Whatever strategies you, your partner, and the "other" natural parent decide upon in order to reduce separation anxiety, you should convey to the children that their relationship with their other parent is an important issue for you as well as for them.

## What to Do if a Child Tries to Sabotage Your Wedding Plans

The more emotional security you can provide for children prior to a new marriage, and the more opportunity a prospective step-parent has to develop a supportive relationship, the less it is likely that a child will attempt a major rebellion to halt or delay the wedding plans. However, if children do 'act out' to draw attention to their anxiety and displeasure over the imminent marriage, it is generally wise to proceed according to schedule.

Though you want to be very sensitive to your natural or step-child's fear of change, there are important reasons why you should avoid capitulating to sabotage attempts on the part of children. It is extremely unwise to make a child believe that he or she is that powerful.

Children need to believe that parents can set limits on their tantrums and other destructive behavior. They can't feel protected, secure, and loved (or even that they are lovable) when they believe they can control major areas of a parent's life.

Another serious side effect of letting children become successful in halting or delaying wedding plans is that is makes them triumphant rivals over someone else their parent loves. Rather than learning that love can be shared without loss to anyone in caring families, children come to believe that they are entitled to full possession of a parent, which can have serious future consequences for their development.

A third major disadvantage of giving in to acting-out children is that they are ultimately denied the strength and support they will gain from having a happy, fulfilled parent with the courage to live out his or her dreams. *The gift of a parent's own happiness is one of the greatest gifts that can ever be given to a child.* A parent's fulfillment as an adult provides one of the most important incentives for children to become mature themselves. Despite many cultural temptations to regress, the proof of a parent's joy and fulfillment is an ever-present reminder that the pain of growing up is worth it.

Because a mature, fulfilled parent gives a child hope for a similar future, both the parent and prospective step-parent should seek to draw the rebellious child into the harmony of their relationship as they proceed with their life.

## *New Marriages and the Natural "Other" Parent*

Adjustment problems with children (whether you are a natural parent, a step-parent or both) in a prospective new marriage are, in some cases, exacerbated if not actually caused by a former spouse, the other natural parent. This is extremely painful and frustrating for the new couple because they have very little control over the behavior of the "other" parent, yet these influences upon the children can seriously affect their lives.

Attempts by a former spouse to control a new marriage by using the children as pawns can vary widely from case to case. Sometimes, for example, children are pressured into refusing to attend the wedding itself. In situations in which the "other" parent has custody, interferences may involve interruptions in visitations.

Even more serious problems involving psychological or physical abuse of children may occasionally occur if the "other" parent uses the children as scapegoats for feelings of rejection or loss of control brought on by the prospect of a former spouse's happiness in a new marriage. In some cases seemingly unrelated crises in children's lives, such as problems in school or destructive behavior, might "coincidentally" erupt as the marriage draws nearer because the child is picking up stress and subtle cues from the "other" parent.

In these cases, depending upon the seriousness or persistence of the problem, legal and/or psychological consultation may be necessary. Despite these pressures, however, you and your partner should, whenever possible, resist all efforts to curtail your wedding plans even if it means simplifying the ceremony and your life-style following the marriage in order to turn your simultaneous efforts toward strategies designed to protect the children and facilitate their adjustment.

## *Transitional Problems with Children Require Mutual Commitment*

Needless to say, serious adjustment problems with children, especially if they involve the "other" parent as well, serve as an example of one of the most difficult ways to begin a marriage. Unlike cases involving adult relatives, children truly need the attention and protection of parents, and can't be put "on hold" while you try to live "happily ever after."

Regardless of whether one or both of you have children from previous marriages who are demonstrating adjustment problems, you will have to work together as a dedicated team, often in consultation with mental health specialists, to put order, health, and harmony into your own life and theirs. It's not easy, but couples with real-world—not fairy tale—expectations are capable of doing so, if they are fully committed to the undertaking.

It is very important, however, to be sure of the extent of your respective commitments to this process. If you have reservations about beginning a marriage with difficult transitional problems, or if you sense that your partner has second thoughts, you risk hurting yourself and others badly if you do not bring this issue out into the open. Marriage plans should definitely be put on hold in this case while you mutually explore the dilemma of whether to continue or to terminate the relationship.

## *Assessing Children's Problems in Light of Your Skills and Coping Strategies*

The seriousness of children's maladjustments is also a consideration in determining whether you or your partner are capable enough or motivated enough to face the problem together. Some children, for example, may demonstrate mild problems which can be easily alleviated with time and appropriate interventions. For example, young children experiencing stress frequently demonstrate sudden changes in behavior such as fist-fighting for the first time on the playground or becoming afraid of the dark.

Older children tend to demonstrate social role changes. For example, grades of a high achiever may suddenly plummet over several marking periods; the adolescent may become either more aggressive or more insecure with adults and peers; or a formerly well-groomed youngster might suddenly start wearing tee-shirts with toilets on the front and double entendres on the back.

Relatively mild cases generally present little difficulty to couples experienced in child behavior, because stresses other than remarriage can trigger behavior changes. Psychological consultation may be helpful in designing approaches to help children through a difficult adjustment period. In other cases, more serious problems may have been brewing for a long time which are exacerbated by stressful changes surrounding remarriage.

Fire-setting in younger children or drug addiction in adolescents are examples of very serious problems which have enormous ramifications upon the lives of parents and step-parents. Very serious cases in which children's destructive behavior endangers their own lives or those of others may make it more important for parents to "put their own house in order" before attempting to undertake a marriage. In any case, when destructive behavior is serious, both partners need to consult professionals with expertise in maladjusted behavior in children. Severe difficulties in children's behavior entail enormous responsibilities on the part of parents and prospective step-parents. The consequences of these problems need to be explored in depth with a competent professional before couples attempt beginning a new life together.

Whether adjustment problems of children are relatively mild or very severe, whether they involve the children alone, or the contributing dynamics of an ex-spouse: if you are tempted to enter into a marital union out of a sense of duty or guilt, or put such a "trip" on your partner in order to progress toward marriage, you will be setting yourself up for tragedy on a grand scale. It should be immediately obvious that if you are having problems with children *before* you enter into a guilt-ridden, half-hearted marriage, you can be sure that this will be a mere drop in the bucket compared to what you will face in the future.

On the other hand, partners who feel strongly about their love for one another as well as their commitment to the children who will share their relationship, tend to see challenges in helping their children adjust as opportunities. A committed, loving relationship between two competent adults provides a framework for parents to turn their own lives around, as well as those of the most important people in the world to them (next to their respective partners)—their children.

## *New Marriages, Old Problems: More Pro's than Con's in Facing Them Together*

While we don't wish difficult transitional problems on any engaged couple, an opportunity to turn a bleak future for you and your children or step-children into a blossoming one is well worth undertaking if you are resolved to see it through. The early years may be tough in spite of your love for one another, but your investment can create a future worth waiting for. Your joy in one another can help sustain you through heartaches and frustrations as you seek to repair the damage to your children. In the process, the challenges involved make it necessary to each of you to tap into your strengths and develop great trust in yourselves and your relationship.

Courage, responsibility, integrity and trust are important assets for partners in any successful marriage. Couples who have resolved to make their own lives better by working through children's problems with maturity and dedication, tend to end up with double doses of these qualities and to double the amount of love that goes with them. Pulling together to help yourselves and your children through difficult adjustments due to old injuries and the stress of change is a courageous undertaking, but it can be quite an emotionally rewarding experience as well.

# Chapter Sixteen

## THE BIG DAY: YOUR MARRIAGE CEREMONY

### *Make Your Wedding Unique*

A somewhat cynical bachelor acquaintance once remarked, "If I ever get married, I'll do it by just going down to City Hall during my lunch hour." There are *two* excellent reasons why you should *not* take this casual approach to your wedding. You certainly don't have to hold an expensive, lavish affair if that isn't your style, but you and your mate deserve a *meaningful, unique experience* on the occasion of exchanging vows—something you can remember fondly for your entire lives.

First of all, a wedding is not only a public declaration of love but also an expression of pride and confidence in one another. You are making a profound commitment and accepting a far-reaching responsibility. It is important for you and your families to realize the full significance of your vows to each other and the certainty you both feel that these promises can be kept. The ceremony, then, is an act of affirmation and reassurance to each other and to all the people you love. It is also a time for sharing your overflowing happiness with others.

A wedding is also a *rite of passage*. Like a graduation, it marks your transition into a more mature phase of life. In addition, it is a celebration of *achievement*. You have, after all, put enormous effort into finding a suitable mate. Now it is time for everyone to appreciate that effort and rejoice with you. Reward yourself. Make your wedding special!

Whether you finally choose a traditional service or write your own, it's time to concentrate on the beauty and meaning of the words and symbols which will unite you.

## Ron and Ingrid See Their Dream Become Reality

Ron and Ingrid decided to hold their wedding in the Unitarian Church which Ingrid attended. In collaboration with the minister, they adapted the traditional wedding service to reflect their own individual tastes and concerns. To keep the occasion intimate, they invited only their closest relatives and a few longtime friends. On a sunny day in May, Ron and Ingrid finally found themselves joyfully facing the altar.

The minister began by reminding the couple of St. Paul's famous definition of true love, taken from First Corinthians, Chapter 12:

> Love suffers long and is kind; love does not envy; love does not parade itself, is not puffed up;
> Does not behave rudely, does not seek its own, is not provoked, thinks no evil;
> Does not rejoice in iniquity, but rejoices in the truth;
> Bears all things, believes all things, hopes all things, endures all things.
> Love never fails . . .
> And now abide faith, hope, love, these three; but the greatest of these is love.

When asked for their vows, Ron and Ingrid promised to "love, honor, and cherish" each other and exchanged rings as an affirmation of their commitment. Following the minister's declaration that the couple were now husband and wife, they kissed gently, then turned to listen to the readings of their chosen family representatives.

Ron's sister read Shakespeare's love sonnet 116:

> Let me not to the marriage of true minds
> Admit impediments. Love is not love
> Which alters when it alteration finds,
> Or bends with the remover to remove:

178

O, no! It is an ever-fixed mark
That looks on tempests and is never shaken;
It is the star to every wand'ring bark,
Whose worth's unknown, although his height be taken.
Love's not time's fool, though rosy lips and cheeks
Within his bending sickle's compass come;
Love alters not with his brief hours and weeks,
But bears it out even to the edge of doom.
    If this be error and upon me prov'd,
    I never writ, nor no man ever lov'd.

Ingrid's brother spoke next, choosing a passage from Donne's charming love poem, "The Good Morrow":

And now good morrow to our waking souls,
    Which watch not one another out of fear;
For love, all love of other sights controls,
    And makes one little room an every where.
Let sea-discoverers to new worlds have gone,
Let maps to others, worlds on worlds have shown,
Let us possess one world, each hath one, and is one.

My face in thine eye, thine in mine appears,
    And true plain hearts do in the faces rest,
Where can we find two better hemispheres
    Without sharp north, without declining west?
What ever dies, was not mixed equally;
If our two loves be one, or, thou and I
Love so alike, that none do slacken, none can die.

Upon the conclustion of their readings, Ron's sister and Ingrid's brother came forward as representatives of their families and accepted unlighted candles from the minister to signify approval of the new relationship. They in turn gave two candles to the bride and groom, who lighted them from a central burning candle on the altar. Candles were then distributed to each of the couple's relatives, including little Donna the flower girl and Ingrid's young nephew. One by one, Ron lighted the candles held out by all the members of Ingrid's family and she lighted the candles held out by all the members of his family. The minister addressed the last words of the ceremony to Ron and Ingrid:

> The lighting of these candles symbolizes your acceptance of your new bonds and responsibilities to each other and to your families. These candles also represent the blessings and good will of countless generations of your families, which we now unite.

Carrying their candles, Ron and Ingrid left the church followed by their families and friends. They felt happily dazed, but they were aware nevertheless of a deep sense of completion. As Ron's father wiped his tears and tried to give his son a hearty slap on the back, he commented: "You two sure know how to do things right!"

Donna agreed. "When I get married," she announced thoughtfully, "I'm going to have a wedding just like this one!"

Ron and Ingrid laughed affectionately as they posed for pictures on the church steps. They hadn't planned to inaugurate a family tradition— but perhaps, unknowingly, they had.

# Chapter Seventeen

## LIVING HAPPILY EVER AFTER

### *No Fairy Tale: Why Perpetual Happiness Is Possible*

As Ron and Ingrid will discover over a long period of time, living "happily ever after" is not a myth but a reality that any devoted couple can achieve. They will certainly encounter problems, struggles, and crises, as do all people in the course of a full life, but their commitment and comforting of each other will enable them to meet these challenges, and even to emerge the richer for it. Any healthy ongoing relationship, especially such an intimate one, is characterized by openness, mutuality, and nurturing. Ideally, a married couple are *best friends*.

The partners in a happy marriage can rely upon one another, confide in one another, and help each other realize the full potential of their talents and personalities. Each watches over the partner's health and well-being; each tries to encourage the partner's maximum development. They provide inspiration and support. By turns, they are guides and therapists to one another. But above all, they are friends, lifetime friends.

### *Falling in Love for the Last Time: A Renewable Experience*

The incomparable experience of falling in love is one few people want to miss. Poets and ordinary mortals like ourselves have elevated it to the rank of a supreme human experience, one that (so everyone wishes) could last forever. Is remaining in love possible in a monogamous, permanent relationship? Cynics say that romance ends with the end of the honeymoon, with the onset of the humdrum daily realities of a life lived in common. This widespread notion presumes that familiarity breeds dullness or, worse, contempt. Actually, marital lifelessness only results when one or both partners stops growing emotionally and spiritually.

In the case of a creative, growing couple, just the reverse is true. Intimacy provides the support system for each partner to develop exciting, new facets of personality. Ron and Ingrid will love each other all the more, in a different way, when they share the experience of becoming parents together and raising children. Each will also love the other's excitement upon mastering a new hobby, tackling a difficult home improvement project, being rewarded for a bright idea at work, acquiring a fresh insight into themselves; in short, there will be no end to the *newness* of their experiences of loving and sharing as their marriage deepens with the passing years.

In effect, Ron and Ingrid will fall in love again and again—not with different partners but with the different dimensions of personality the adventure of maturing together will bring. They will welcome and revel in the positive changes in each other as their marriage ripens. Their special friendship will confirm the truth of Browning's great lines on such a marriage:

> Grow old along with me—
> The best is yet to be.

True union does not occur instantly; it is gradual. We discover ourselves and bestow ourselves a fraction at a time. Partners are really married by degrees or portions: now a small portion, then a large portion. Only a rare few are ever married completely, and then perhaps only after a half-century of growing together. A total union needs time for mellowing, a lifetime of shared experiences. The Golden Anniversary of Ron and Ingrid is far off, but they can look forward confidently toward the achievement of this rare marriage of perfect union, perfect concord.

Because you and your partner have chosen each other wisely, you also can enjoy the priceless blessing of a happy marriage now and anticipate in the years to come a lifetime of unending fruitfulness. It's not quite correct to say that you have fallen in love for the last time. To be precise, you are falling in love today, tomorrow, and forever with the same amazing, inexhaustible personality, your chosen mate.

For a couple to maintain this ultimate intimacy is, in many ways, success in life itself. As you look forward to achieving it, you and your partner may count yourselves supremely blessed.

# About the Authors

NANCY E. SCHAUMBURGER, Ph.D. has enjoyed success in two careers, as a mental health consultant specializing in adult developmental crises and as a professor of English literature. Now a Department Head at Manhattanville College, Dr. Schaumburger has previously worked at Rockland State Psychiatric Hospital and has written on psychological topics for *The New Women's Times, Belles Lettres,* and other publications. A past member of the Council of Mental Health Practitioners and the American Psychological Association, and a former Research Affiliate of the National Association for the Advancement of Psychoanalysis, Dr. Schaumburger has also taught a number of interdisciplinary courses in literature and psychology. She lives in suburban New Jersey with her advertising executive husband and their three children.

---

MARCIA BRINTON, a school psychologist, obtained a Master of Arts degree in psychology from Montclair State College and is currently completing a doctoral program in psychology at New York University. She is a member of the American Psychological Association and the National Organization of School Psychologists. Mrs. Brinton has published research on person perception and gender in *Personality and Social Psychology Bulletin,* and has presented papers on this topic at annual meetings of the American Psychological Association and the Eastern Psychological Association. Formerly a director of a residential special-education center for emotionally disturbed adolescents, Mrs. Brinton has had extensive experience in counseling families in crisis and transition. She is married to a professor of English and computer science, and has two grown children and three step children. The couple have residences in New York and New Jersey.

DO YOU HAVE A FRIEND OR RELATIVE WHO WOULD ENJOY THIS BOOK?

Use the convenient order form below.

---

# Order Form

### Finding, Loving and Marrying Your Lifetime Partner

YES, please send _____ copies (cloth) at $16.95 each _____
_____ copies (paper) at   9.95 each _____

SUBTOTAL

Tax

Tax: (North Carolina only): 5%          Postage & Handling _____
($1.50 first book
.50 each additional book)

TOTAL _____

NAME _____

ADDRESS _____

_____ Zip _____

Send to:   **Tudor Publishers, Inc.**
P.O. Box 3443
Greensboro, NC 27402

*Prices subject to change without notice.*
*Allow 4-6 weeks for delivery.*

**Our Guarantee:**     *You must be completely satisfied or return the book(s) in undamaged condition within 30 days for a full refund.*